Open Sesame!

Password Journal for Kid's Online Accounts

I0187469

Activinotes

Activinotes

DAILY JOURNALS, PLANNERS, NOTEBOOKS AND OTHER BLANK BOOKS

Password Journal

Notes :

Account Name: _____

Website : _____

User I.D. : _____

Email Used : _____

Password : _____

Account Name: _____

Website : _____

User I.D. : _____

Email Used : _____

Password : _____

Notes :

Notes :

Account Name: _____

Website : _____

User I.D. : _____

Email Used : _____

Password : _____

Account Name: _____

Website : _____

User I.D. : _____

Email Used : _____

Password : _____

Notes :

Password Journal

Password Journal

Notes :

Account Name: _____

Website : _____

User I.D. : _____

Email Used : _____

Password : _____

Account Name: _____

Website : _____

User I.D. : _____

Email Used : _____

Password : _____

Notes :

Notes :

Account Name: _____

Website : _____

User I.D. : _____

Email Used : _____

Password : _____

Account Name: _____

Website : _____

User I.D. : _____

Email Used : _____

Password : _____

Notes :

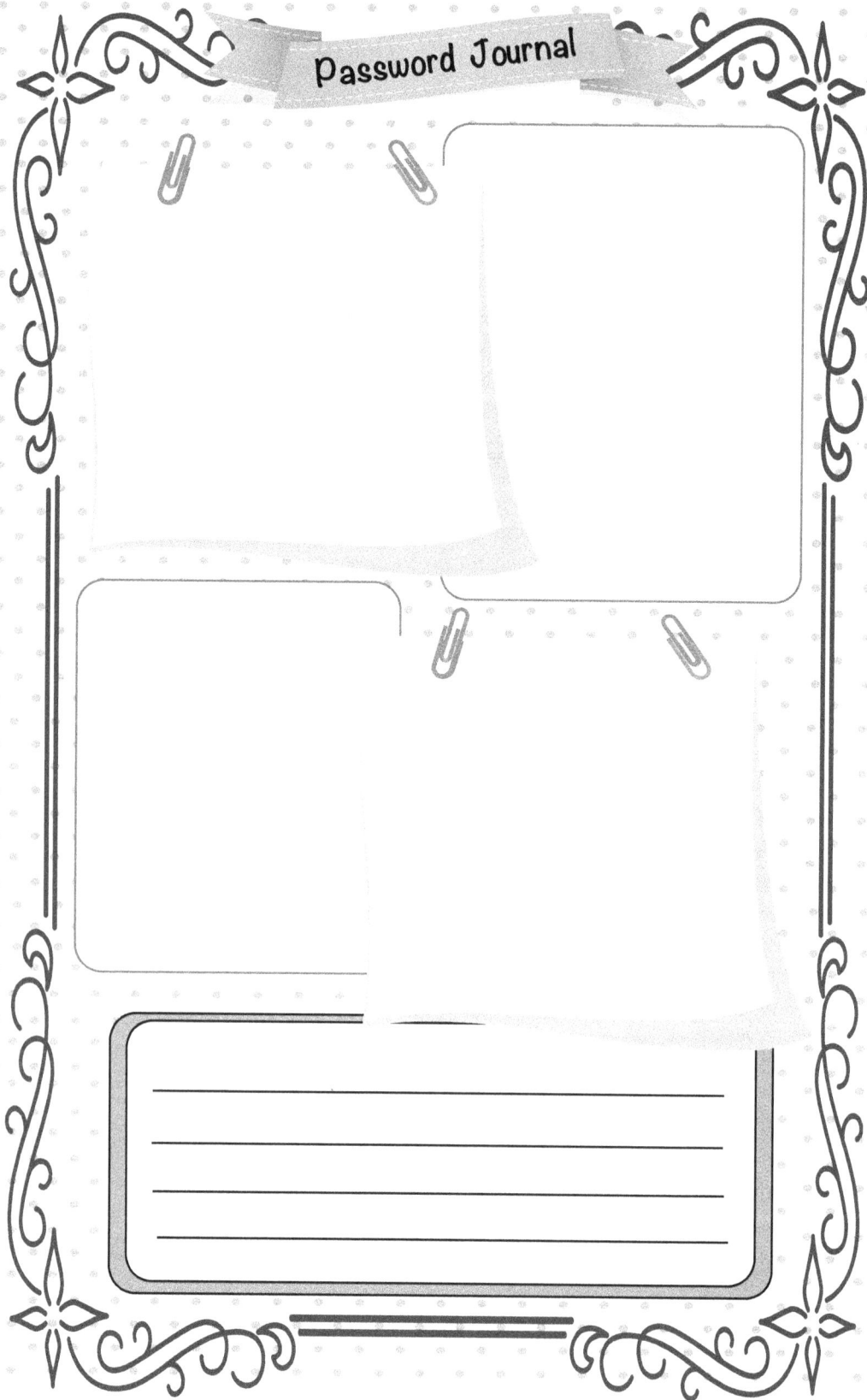

Password Journal

Notes :

Account Name: _____

Website : _____

User I.D. : _____

Email Used : _____

Password : _____

Account Name: _____

Website : _____

User I.D. : _____

Email Used : _____

Password : _____

Notes :

Notes :

Account Name: _____

Website : _____

User I.D. : _____

Email Used : _____

Password : _____

Account Name: _____

Website : _____

User I.D. : _____

Email Used : _____

Password : _____

Notes :

Password Journal

Password Journal

Notes :

Account Name: _____

Website : _____

User I.D. : _____

Email Used : _____

Password : _____

Account Name: _____

Website : _____

User I.D. : _____

Email Used : _____

Password : _____

Notes :

Notes :

Account Name: _____

Website : _____

User I.D. : _____

Email Used : _____

Password : _____

Account Name: _____

Website : _____

User I.D. : _____

Email Used : _____

Password : _____

Notes :

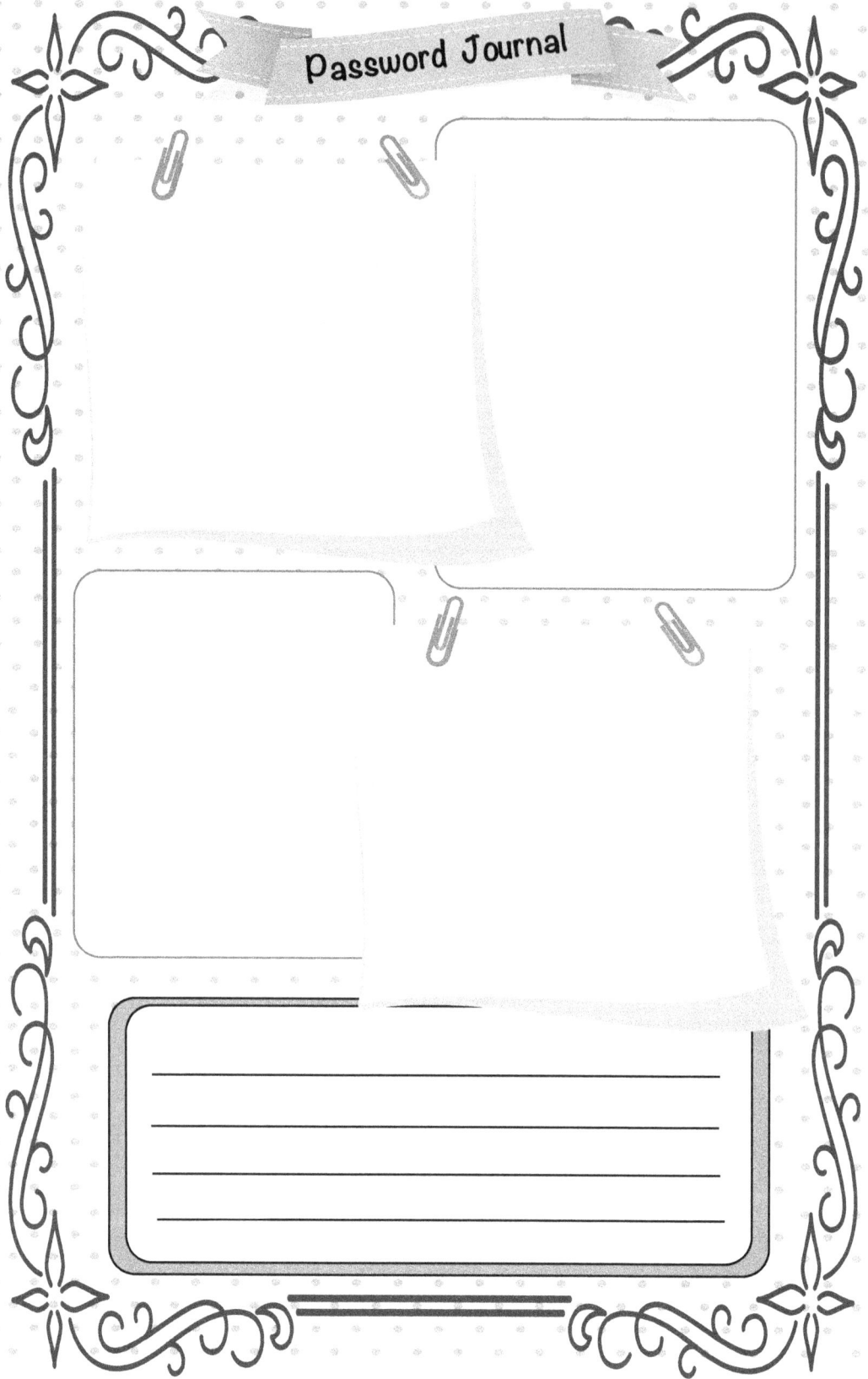

Password Journal

Notes :

Account Name: _____

Website : _____

User I.D. : _____

Email Used : _____

Password : _____

Account Name: _____

Website : _____

User I.D. : _____

Email Used : _____

Password : _____

Notes :

Notes :

Account Name: _____

Website : _____

User I.D. : _____

Email Used : _____

Password : _____

Account Name: _____

Website : _____

User I.D. : _____

Email Used : _____

Password : _____

Notes :

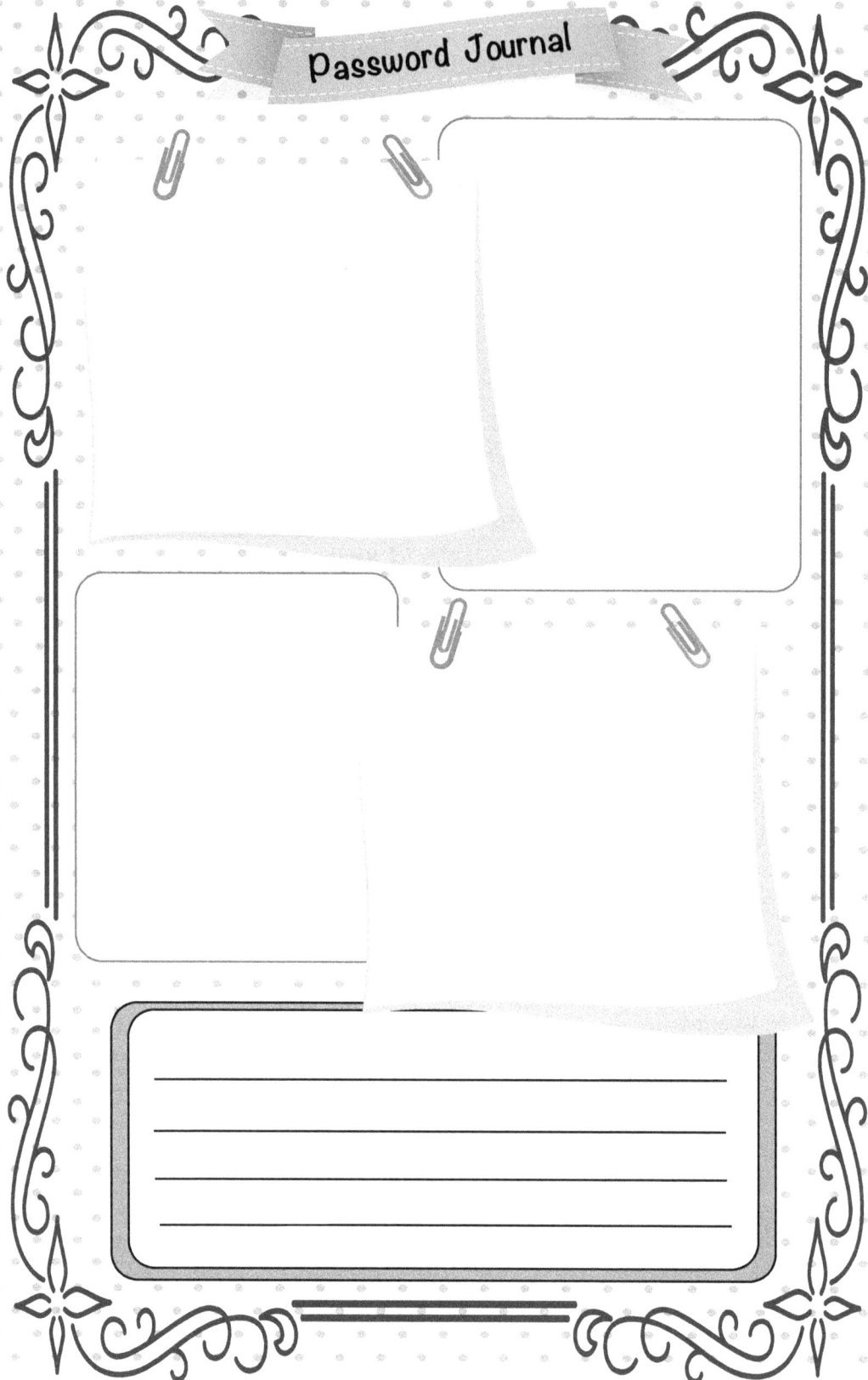

Password Journal

Notes :

Account Name: _____

Website : _____

User I.D. : _____

Email Used : _____

Password : _____

Account Name: _____

Website : _____

User I.D. : _____

Email Used : _____

Password : _____

Notes :

Notes :

Account Name: _____

Website : _____

User I.D. : _____

Email Used : _____

Password : _____

Account Name: _____

Website : _____

User I.D. : _____

Email Used : _____

Password : _____

Notes :

Password Journal

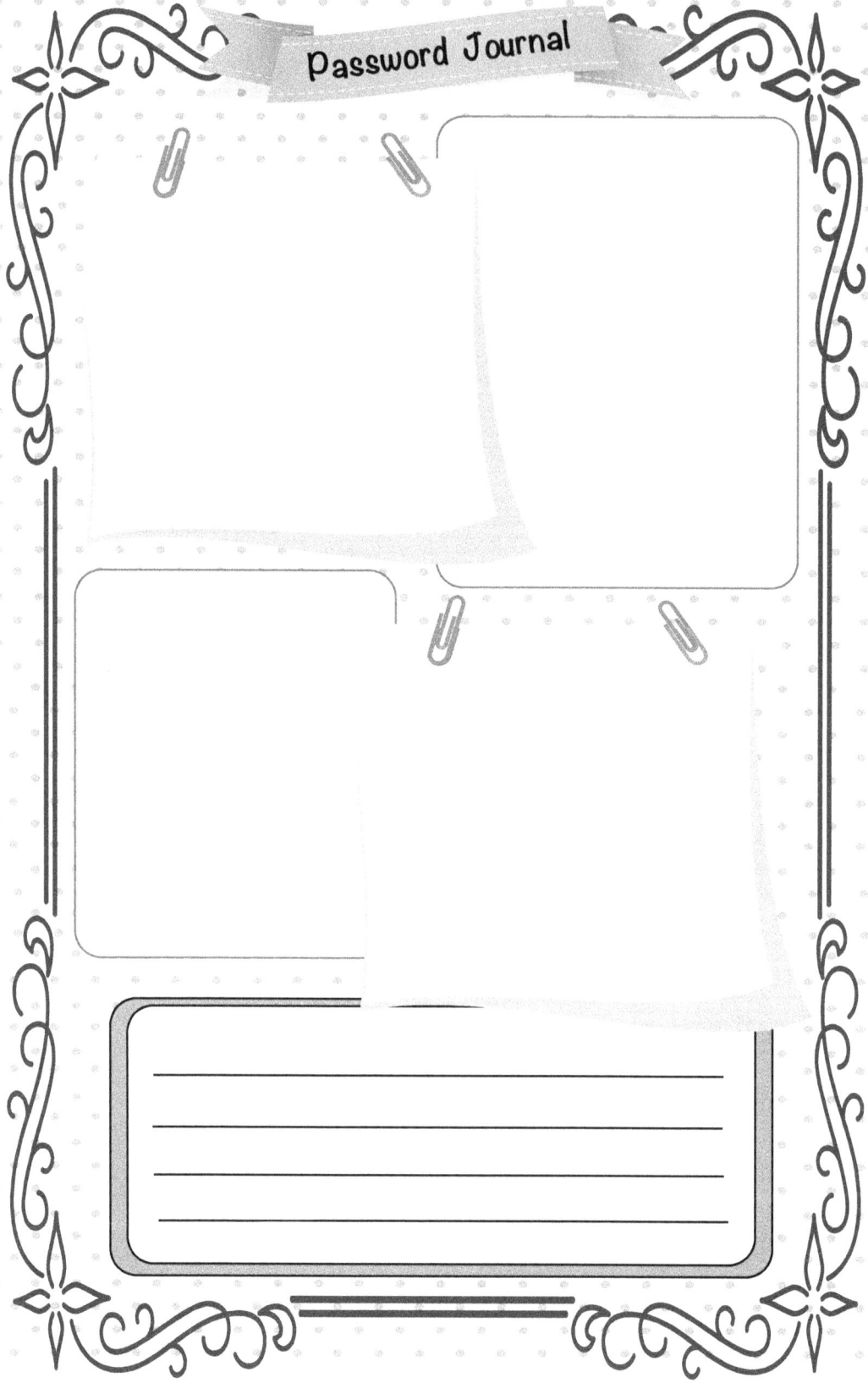

Password Journal

Notes :

Account Name: _____

Website : _____

User I.D. : _____

Email Used : _____

Password : _____

Account Name: _____

Website : _____

User I.D. : _____

Email Used : _____

Password : _____

Notes :

Notes :

Account Name: _____

Website : _____

User I.D. : _____

Email Used : _____

Password : _____

Account Name: _____

Website : _____

User I.D. : _____

Email Used : _____

Password : _____

Notes :

Password Journal

Notes :

Account Name: _____

Website : _____

User I.D. : _____

Email Used : _____

Password : _____

Account Name: _____

Website : _____

User I.D. : _____

Email Used : _____

Password : _____

Notes :

Notes :

Account Name: _____

Website : _____

User I.D. : _____

Email Used : _____

Password : _____

Account Name: _____

Website : _____

User I.D. : _____

Email Used : _____

Password : _____

Notes :

Password Journal

Notes :

Account Name: _____

Website : _____

User I.D. : _____

Email Used : _____

Password : _____

Account Name: _____

Website : _____

User I.D. : _____

Email Used : _____

Password : _____

Notes :

Notes :

Account Name: _____

Website : _____

User I.D. : _____

Email Used : _____

Password : _____

Account Name: _____

Website : _____

User I.D. : _____

Email Used : _____

Password : _____

Notes :

Password Journal

Password Journal

Notes :

Account Name: _____

Website : _____

User I.D. : _____

Email Used : _____

Password : _____

Account Name: _____

Website : _____

User I.D. : _____

Email Used : _____

Password : _____

Notes :

Notes :

Account Name: _____

Website : _____

User I.D. : _____

Email Used : _____

Password : _____

Account Name: _____

Website : _____

User I.D. : _____

Email Used : _____

Password : _____

Notes :

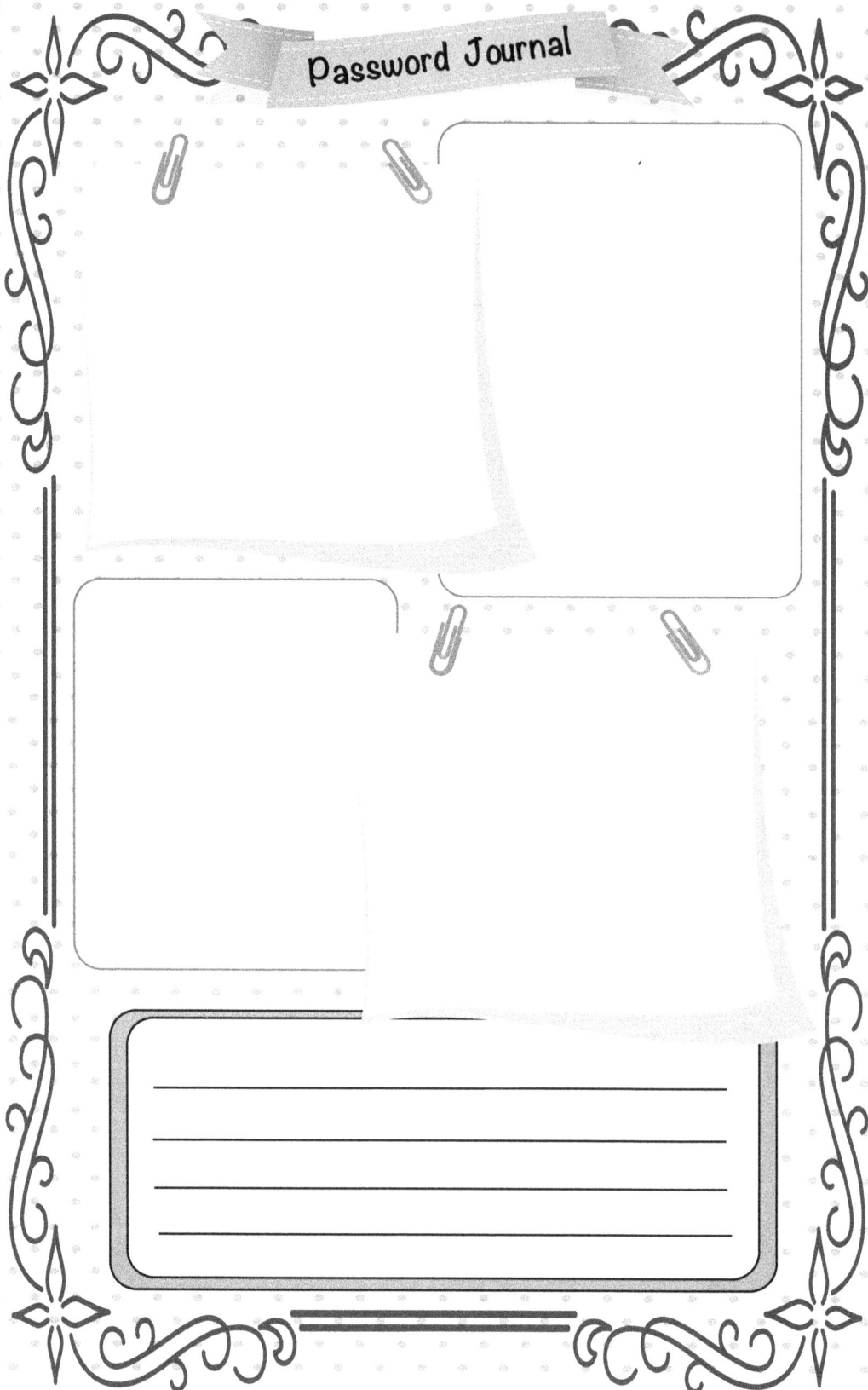

Password Journal

Notes :

Account Name: _____

Website : _____

User I.D. : _____

Email Used : _____

Password : _____

Account Name: _____

Website : _____

User I.D. : _____

Email Used : _____

Password : _____

Notes :

Notes :

Account Name: _____

Website : _____

User I.D. : _____

Email Used : _____

Password : _____

Account Name: _____

Website : _____

User I.D. : _____

Email Used : _____

Password : _____

Notes :

Password Journal

Notes :

Account Name: _____

Website : _____

User I.D. : _____

Email Used : _____

Password : _____

Account Name: _____

Website : _____

User I.D. : _____

Email Used : _____

Password : _____

Notes :

Notes :

Account Name: _____

Website : _____

User I.D. : _____

Email Used : _____

Password : _____

Account Name: _____

Website : _____

User I.D. : _____

Email Used : _____

Password : _____

Notes :

Password Journal

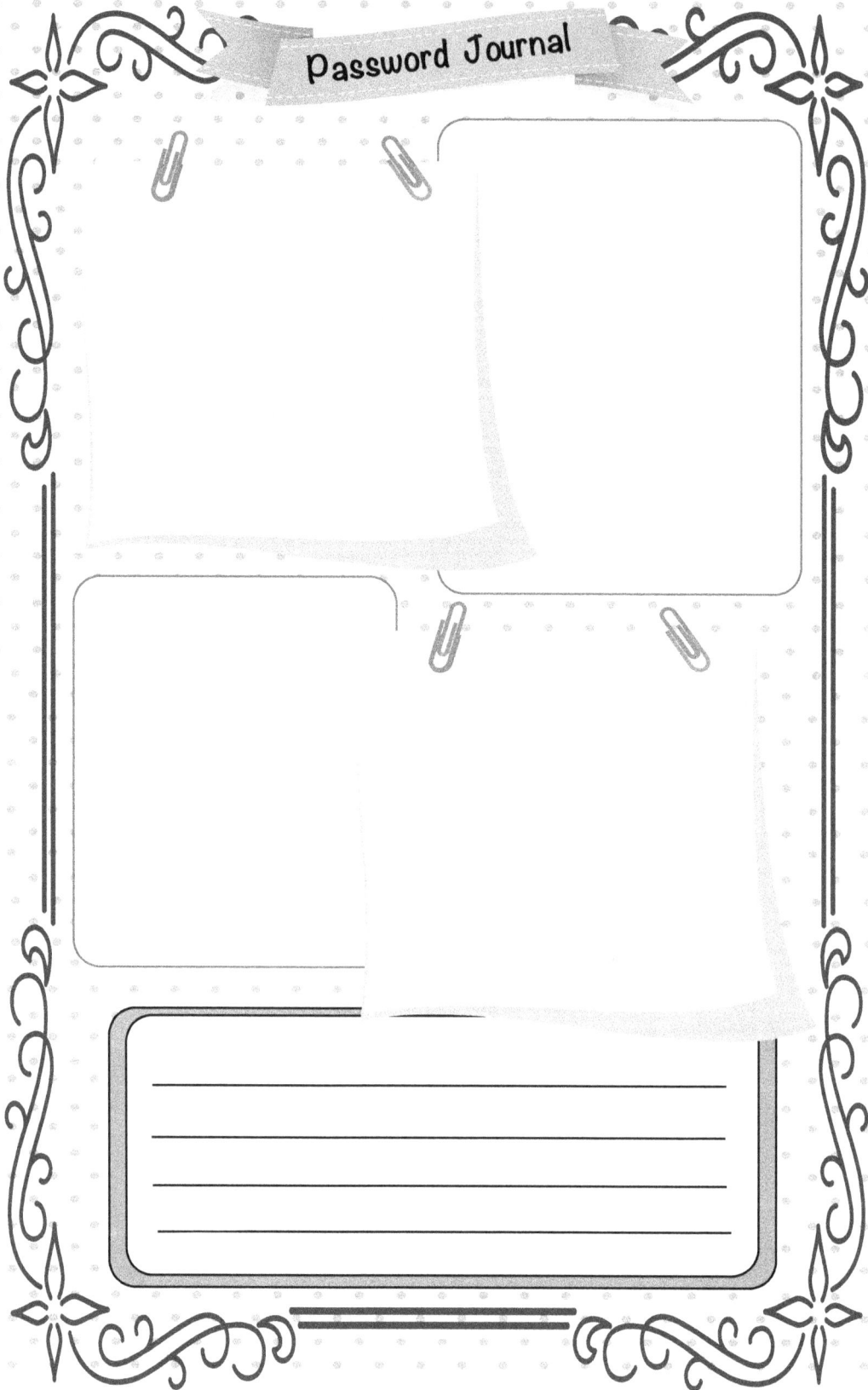

Password Journal

Notes :

Account Name: _____

Website : _____

User I.D. : _____

Email Used : _____

Password : _____

Account Name: _____

Website : _____

User I.D. : _____

Email Used : _____

Password : _____

Notes :

Notes :

Account Name: _____

Website : _____

User I.D. : _____

Email Used : _____

Password : _____

Account Name: _____

Website : _____

User I.D. : _____

Email Used : _____

Password : _____

Notes :

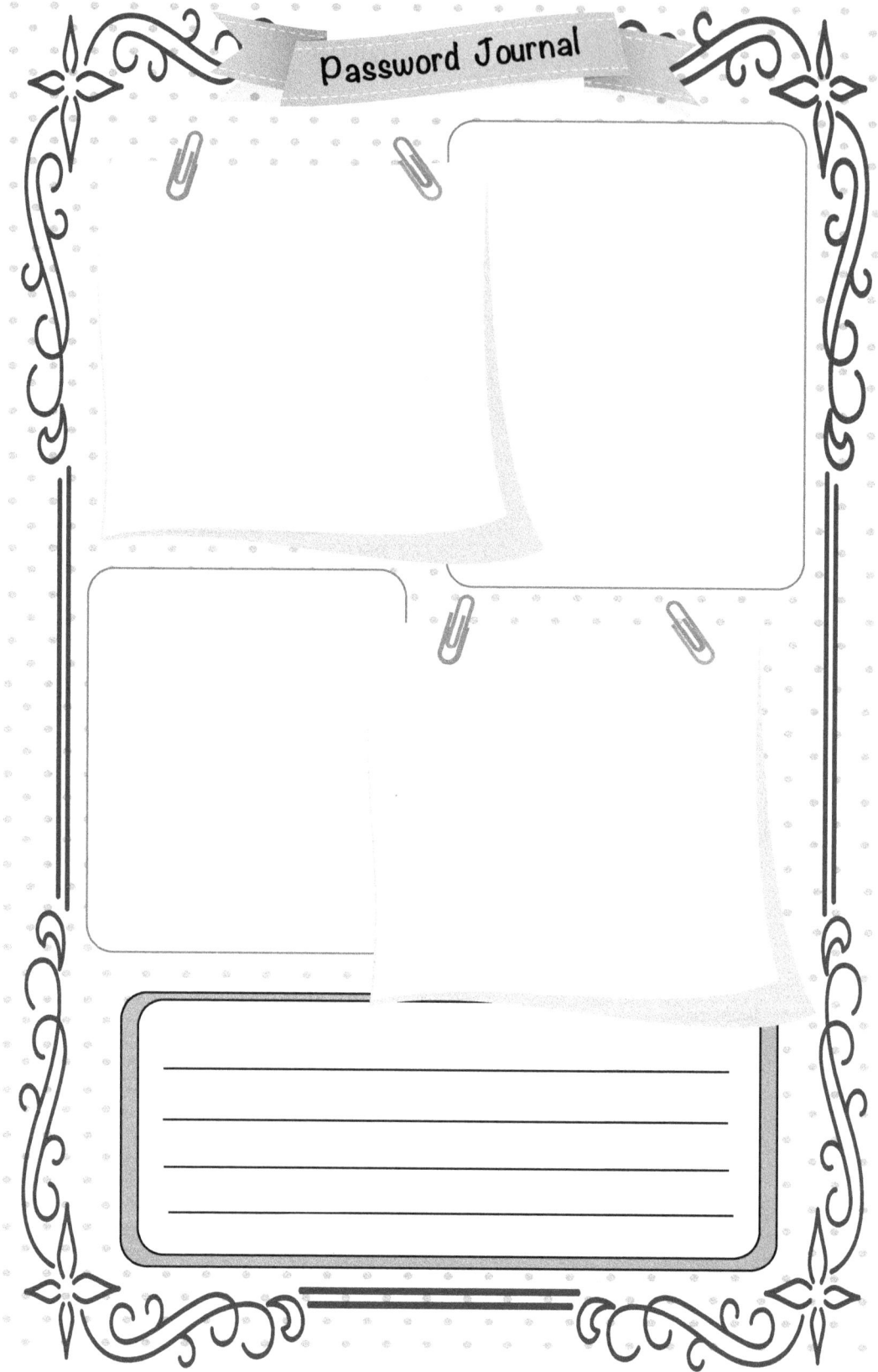

Password Journal

Notes :

Account Name: _____

Website : _____

User I.D. : _____

Email Used : _____

Password : _____

Account Name: _____

Website : _____

User I.D. : _____

Email Used : _____

Password : _____

Notes :

Notes :

Account Name: _____

Website : _____

User I.D. : _____

Email Used : _____

Password : _____

Account Name: _____

Website : _____

User I.D. : _____

Email Used : _____

Password : _____

Notes :

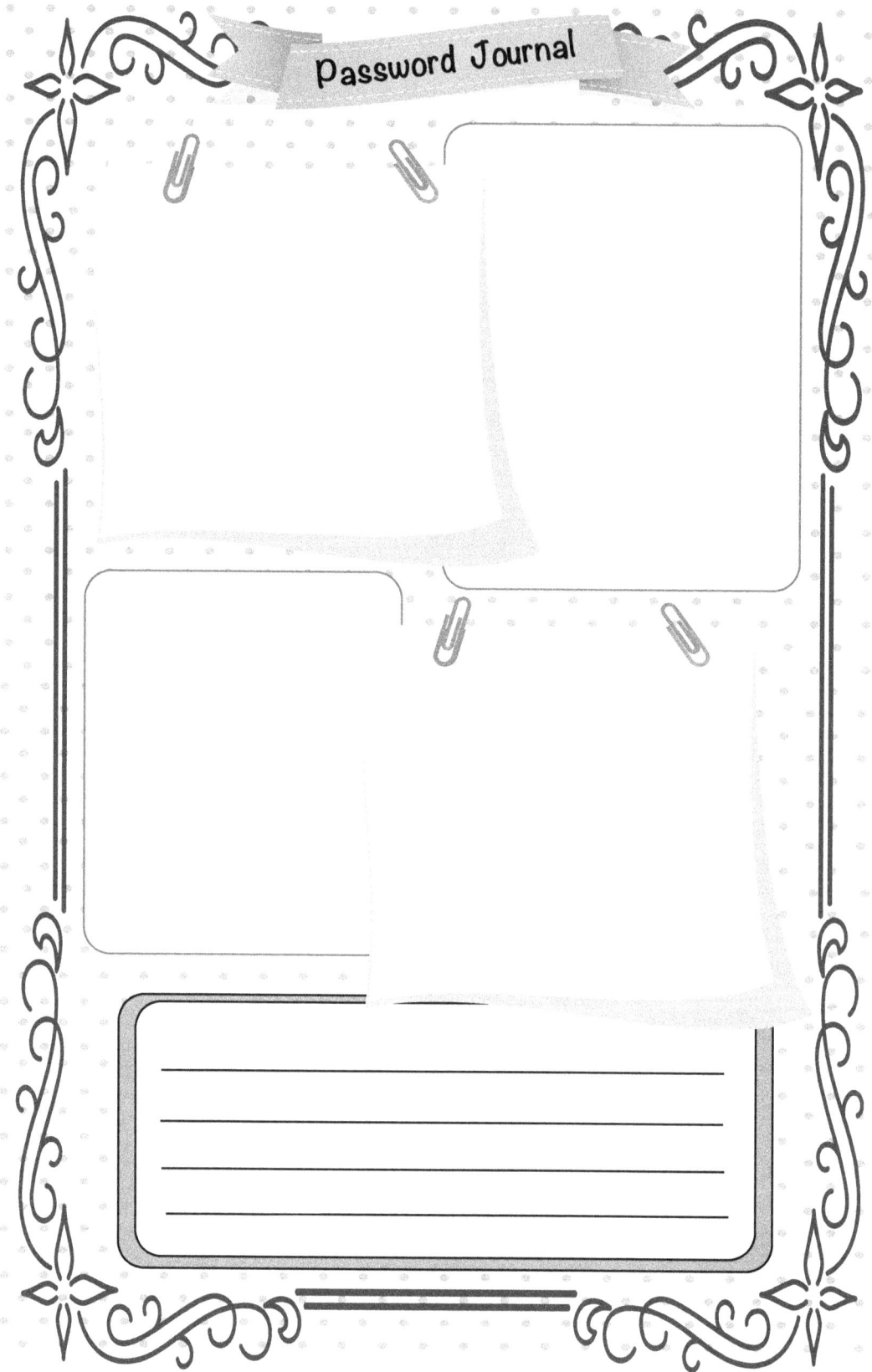

Password Journal

Notes :

Account Name: _____

Website : _____

User I.D. : _____

Email Used : _____

Password : _____

Account Name: _____

Website : _____

User I.D. : _____

Email Used : _____

Password : _____

Notes :

Notes :

Account Name: _____

Website : _____

User I.D. : _____

Email Used : _____

Password : _____

Account Name: _____

Website : _____

User I.D. : _____

Email Used : _____

Password : _____

Notes :

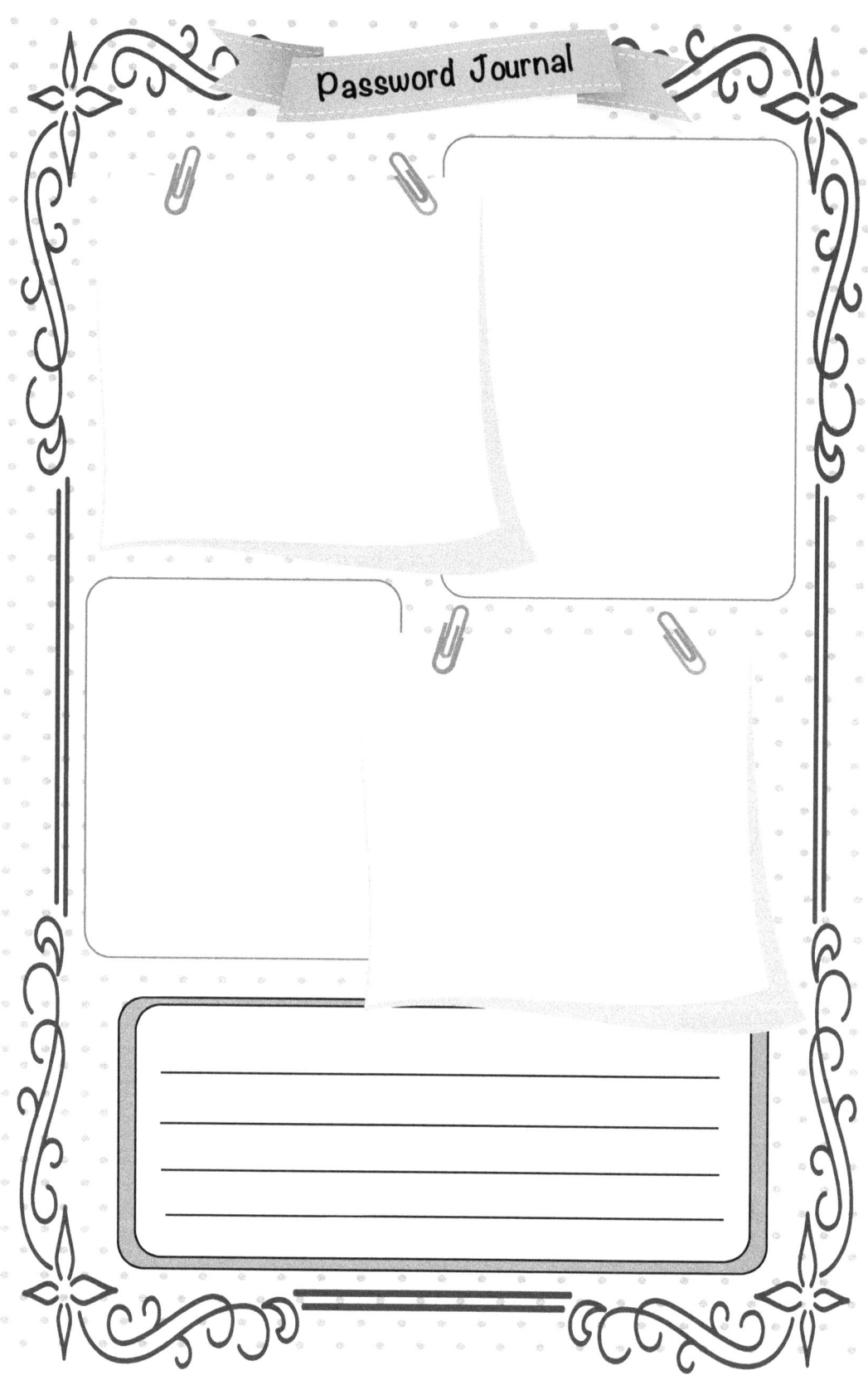

Password Journal

Notes :

Account Name: _____

Website : _____

User I.D. : _____

Email Used : _____

Password : _____

Account Name: _____

Website : _____

User I.D. : _____

Email Used : _____

Password : _____

Notes :

Notes :

Account Name: _____

Website : _____

User I.D. : _____

Email Used : _____

Password : _____

Account Name: _____

Website : _____

User I.D. : _____

Email Used : _____

Password : _____

Notes :

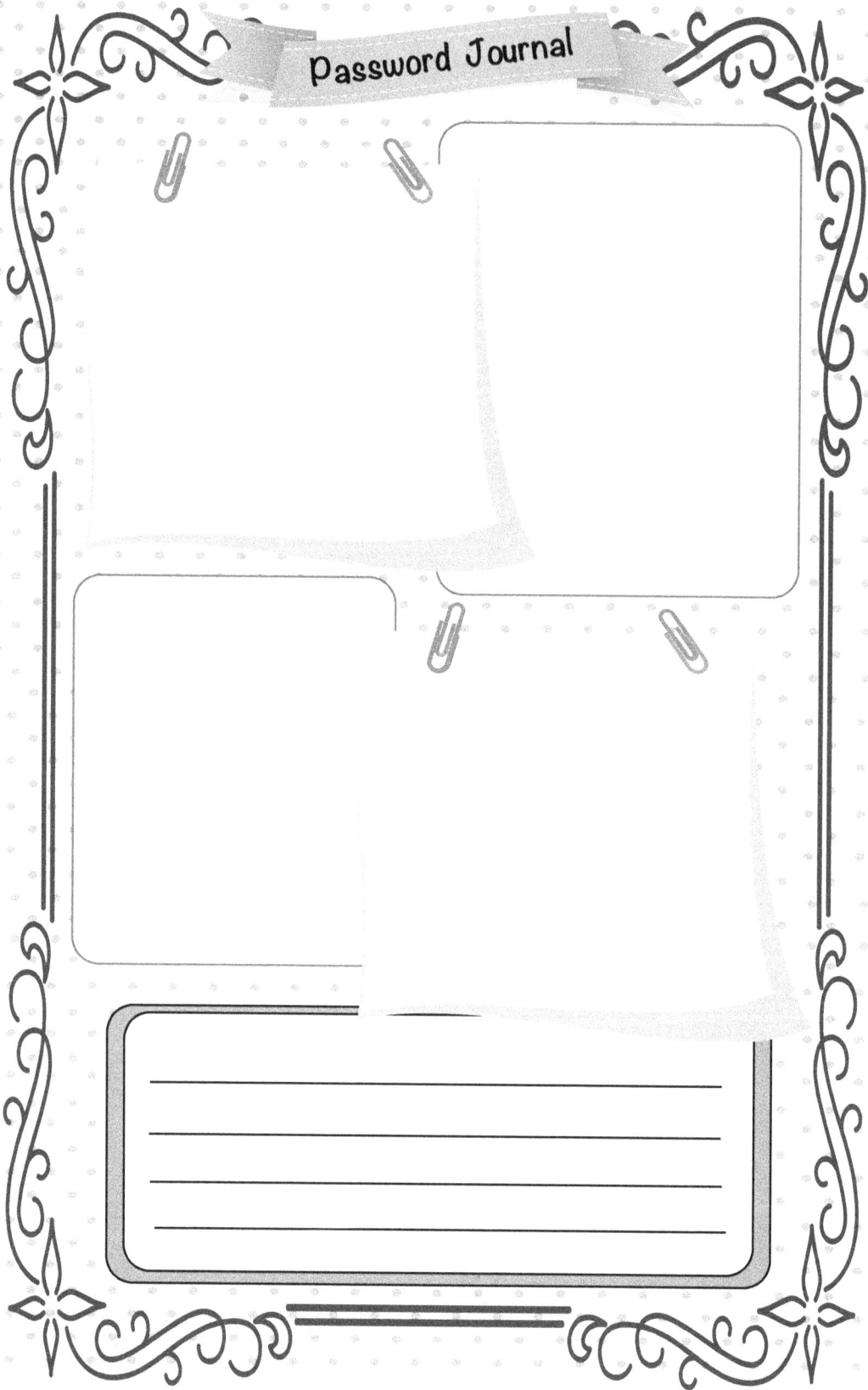

Password Journal

Notes :

Account Name: _____

Website : _____

User I.D. : _____

Email Used : _____

Password : _____

Account Name: _____

Website : _____

User I.D. : _____

Email Used : _____

Password : _____

Notes :

Notes :

Account Name: _____

Website : _____

User I.D. : _____

Email Used : _____

Password : _____

Account Name: _____

Website : _____

User I.D. : _____

Email Used : _____

Password : _____

Notes :

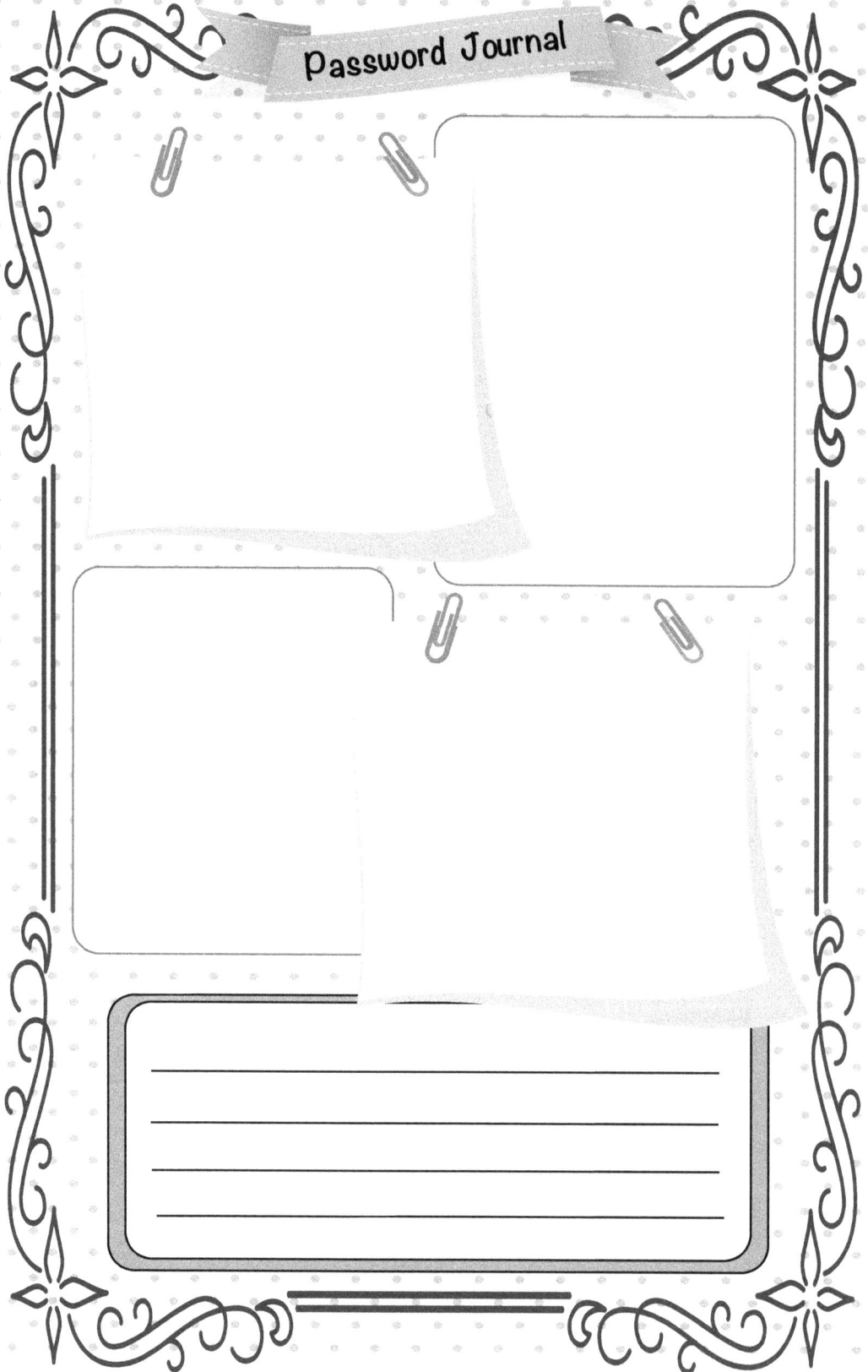

Password Journal

Notes :

Account Name: _____

Website : _____

User I.D. : _____

Email Used : _____

Password : _____

Account Name: _____

Website : _____

User I.D. : _____

Email Used : _____

Password : _____

Notes :

Notes :

Account Name: _____

Website : _____

User I.D. : _____

Email Used : _____

Password : _____

Account Name: _____

Website : _____

User I.D. : _____

Email Used : _____

Password : _____

Notes :

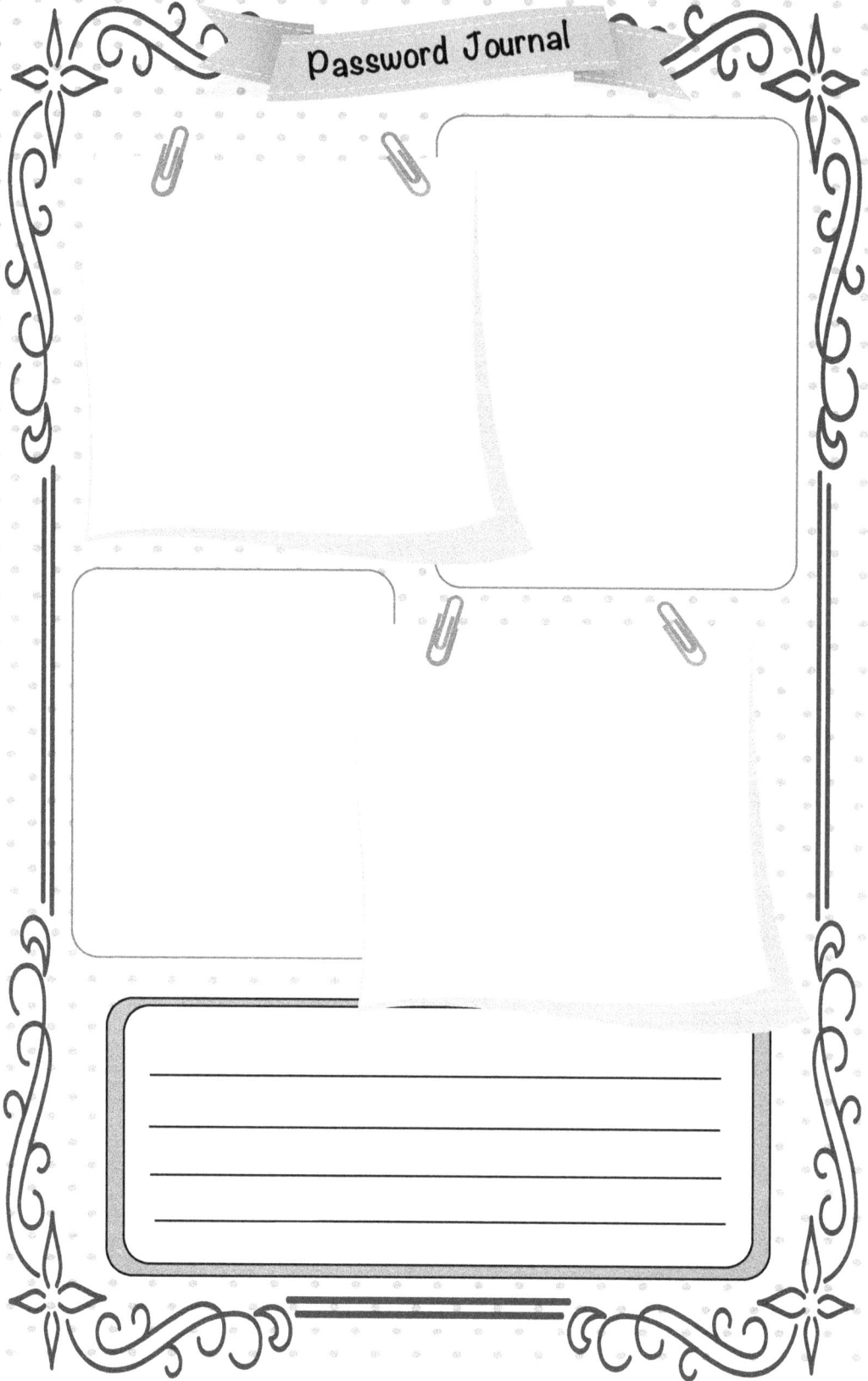

Password Journal

Notes :

Account Name: _____

Website : _____

User I.D. : _____

Email Used : _____

Password : _____

Account Name: _____

Website : _____

User I.D. : _____

Email Used : _____

Password : _____

Notes :

Notes :

Account Name: _____

Website : _____

User I.D. : _____

Email Used : _____

Password : _____

Account Name: _____

Website : _____

User I.D. : _____

Email Used : _____

Password : _____

Notes :

Password Journal

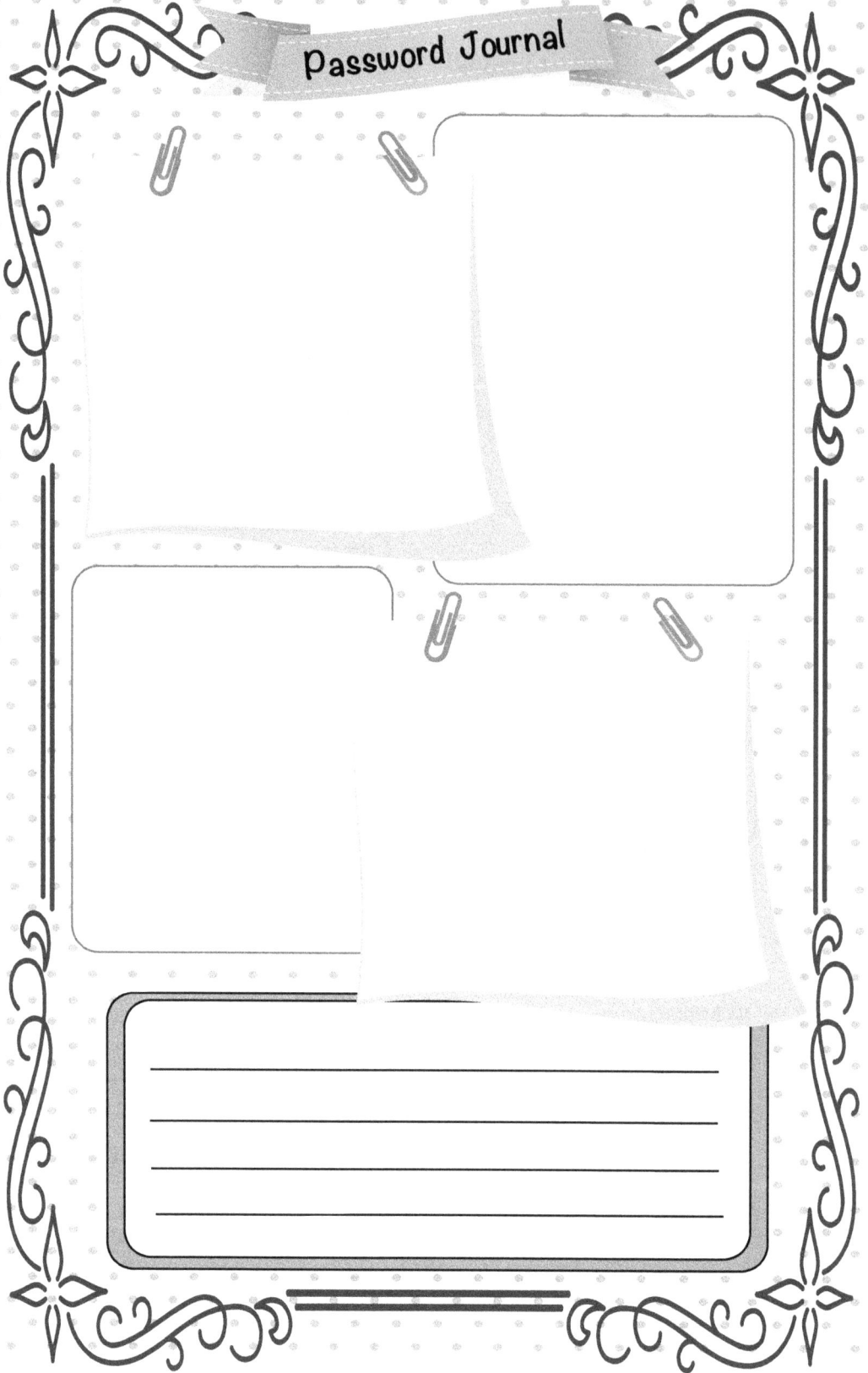

Password Journal

Notes :

Account Name: _____

Website : _____

User I.D. : _____

Email Used : _____

Password : _____

Account Name: _____

Website : _____

User I.D. : _____

Email Used : _____

Password : _____

Notes :

Notes :

Account Name: _____

Website : _____

User I.D. : _____

Email Used : _____

Password : _____

Account Name: _____

Website : _____

User I.D. : _____

Email Used : _____

Password : _____

Notes :

Password Journal

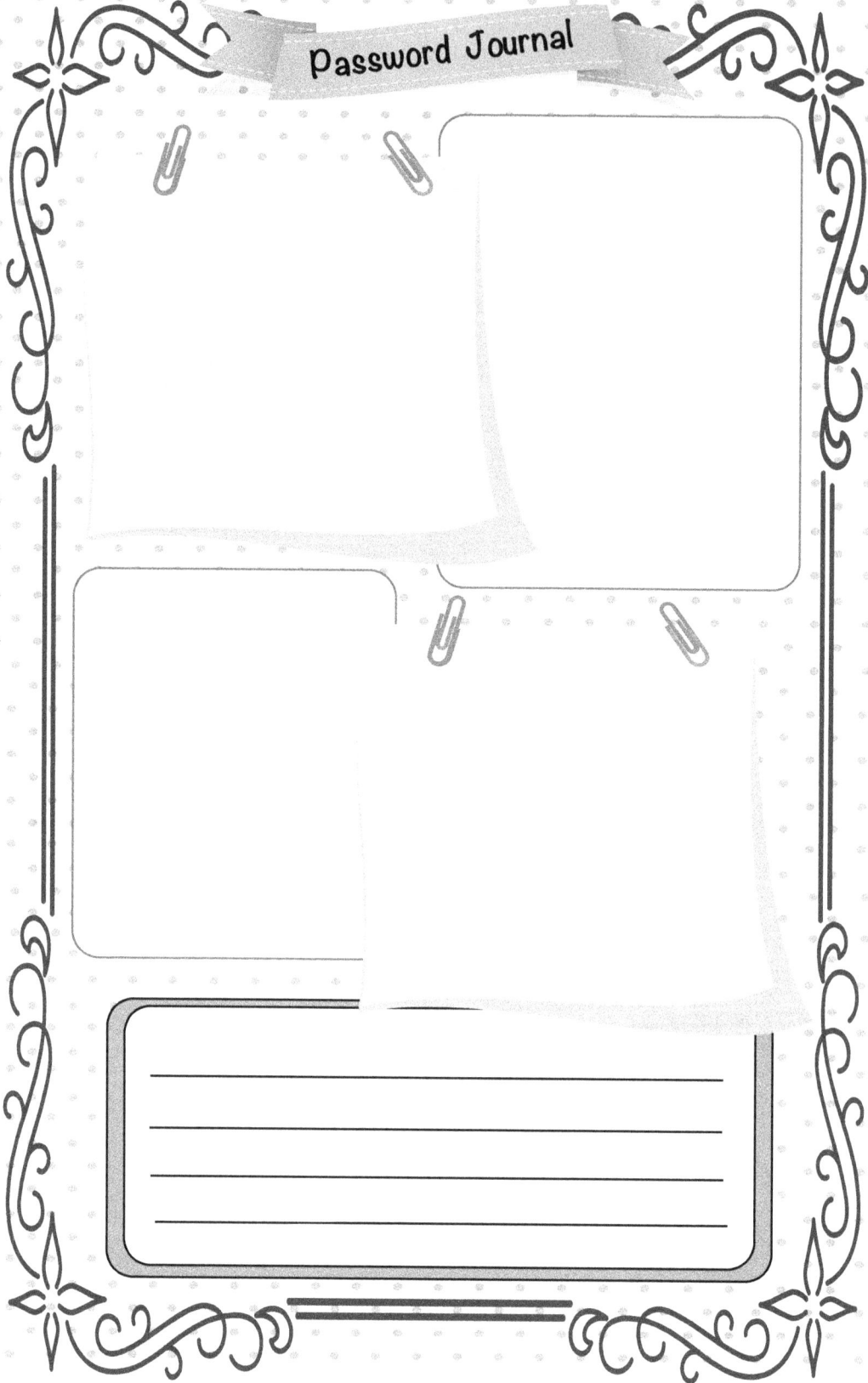

Password Journal

Notes :

Account Name: _____

Website : _____

User I.D. : _____

Email Used : _____

Password : _____

Account Name: _____

Website : _____

User I.D. : _____

Email Used : _____

Password : _____

Notes :

Notes :

Account Name: _____

Website : _____

User I.D. : _____

Email Used : _____

Password : _____

Account Name: _____

Website : _____

User I.D. : _____

Email Used : _____

Password : _____

Notes :

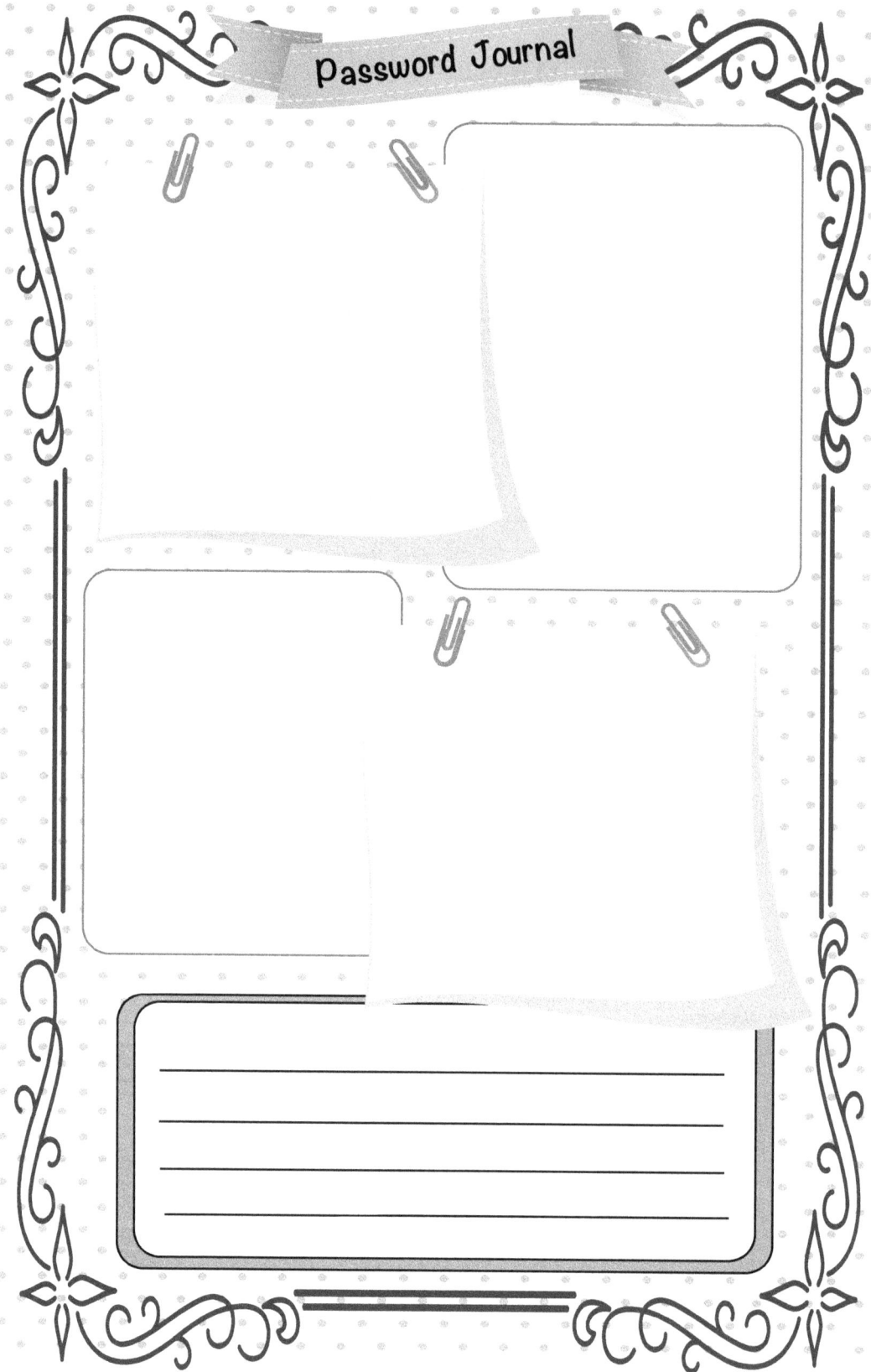

Password Journal

Notes :

Account Name: _____

Website : _____

User I.D. : _____

Email Used : _____

Password : _____

Account Name: _____

Website : _____

User I.D. : _____

Email Used : _____

Password : _____

Notes :

Notes :

Account Name: _____

Website : _____

User I.D. : _____

Email Used : _____

Password : _____

Account Name: _____

Website : _____

User I.D. : _____

Email Used : _____

Password : _____

Notes :

Password Journal

Notes :

Account Name: _____

Website : _____

User I.D. : _____

Email Used : _____

Password : _____

Account Name: _____

Website : _____

User I.D. : _____

Email Used : _____

Password : _____

Notes :

Notes :

Account Name: _____

Website : _____

User I.D. : _____

Email Used : _____

Password : _____

Account Name: _____

Website : _____

User I.D. : _____

Email Used : _____

Password : _____

Notes :

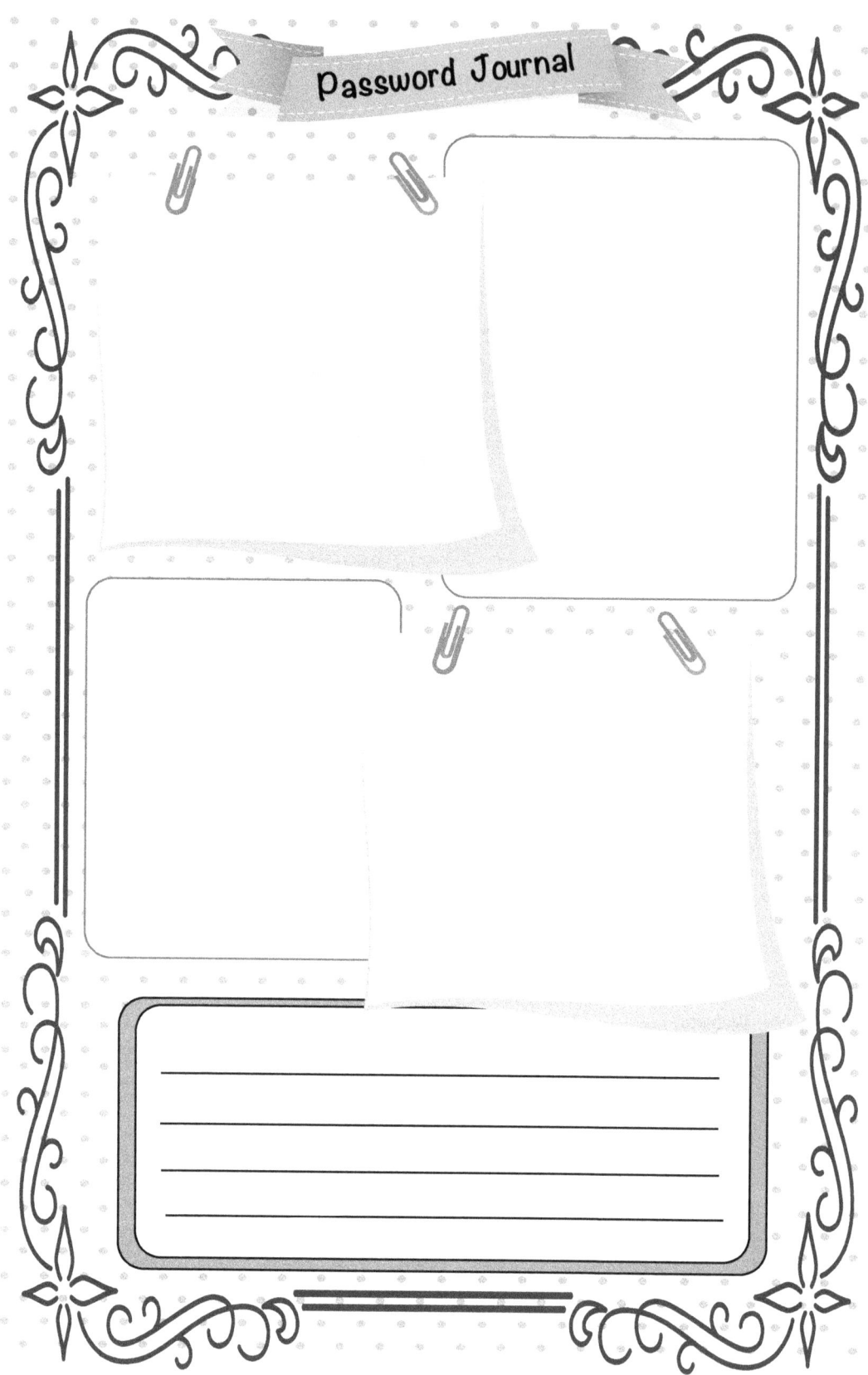

Password Journal

Notes :

Account Name: _____

Website : _____

User I.D. : _____

Email Used : _____

Password : _____

Account Name: _____

Website : _____

User I.D. : _____

Email Used : _____

Password : _____

Notes :

Notes :

Account Name: _____

Website : _____

User I.D. : _____

Email Used : _____

Password : _____

Account Name: _____

Website : _____

User I.D. : _____

Email Used : _____

Password : _____

Notes :

Password Journal

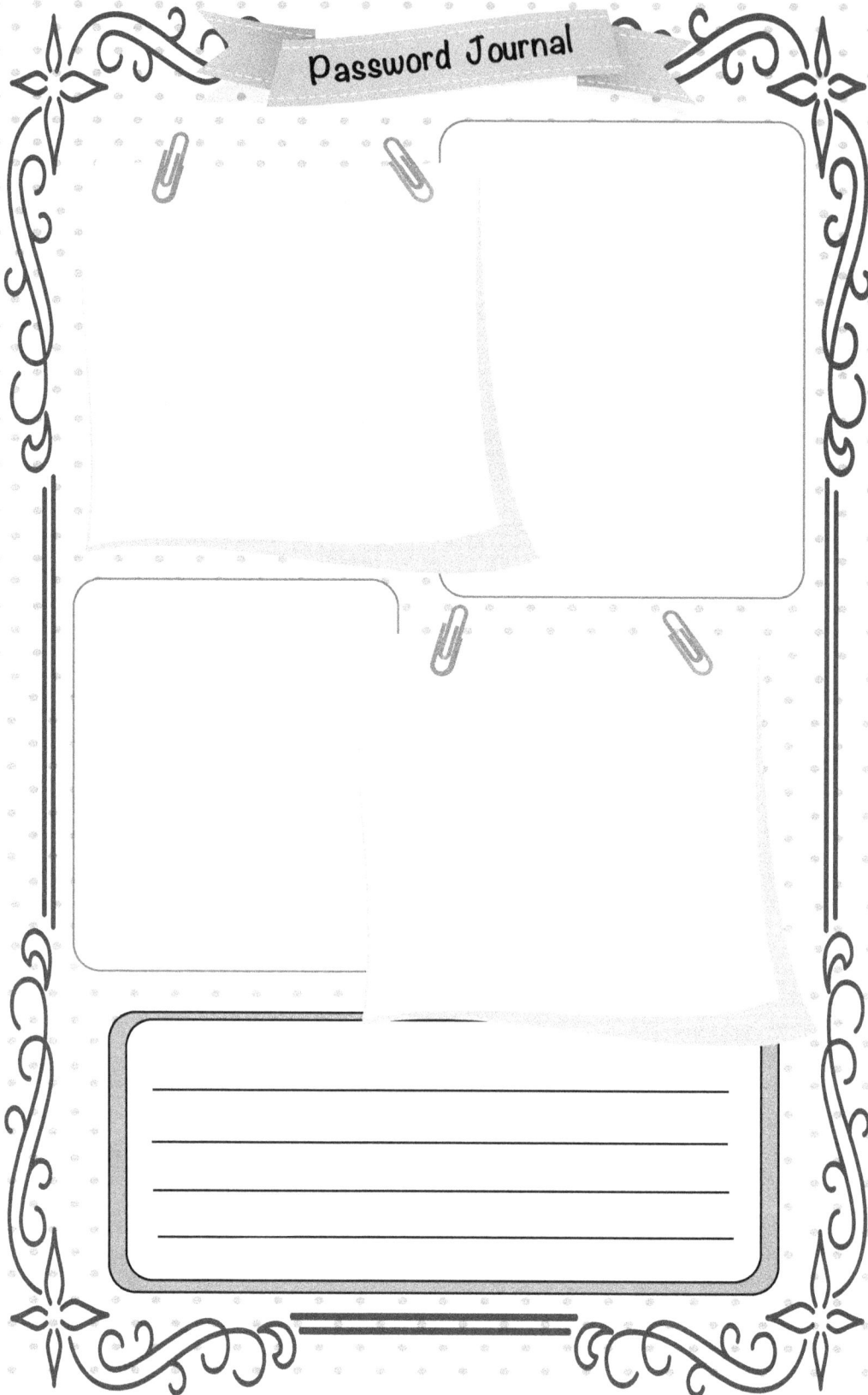

Password Journal

Notes :

Account Name: _____

Website : _____

User I.D. : _____

Email Used : _____

Password : _____

Account Name: _____

Website : _____

User I.D. : _____

Email Used : _____

Password : _____

Notes :

Notes :

Account Name: _____

Website : _____

User I.D. : _____

Email Used : _____

Password : _____

Account Name: _____

Website : _____

User I.D. : _____

Email Used : _____

Password : _____

Notes :

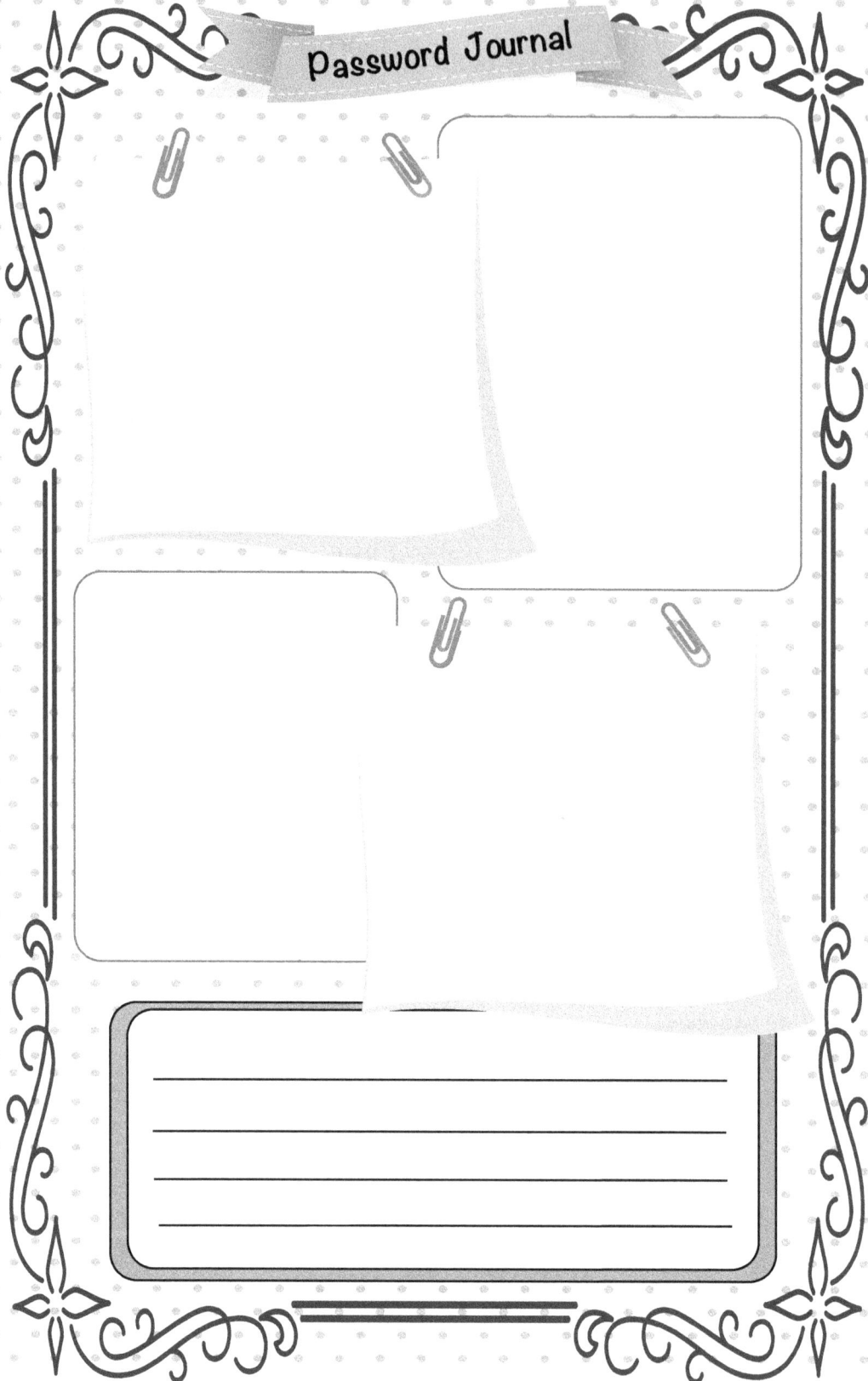

Password Journal

Notes :

Account Name: _____

Website : _____

User I.D. : _____

Email Used : _____

Password : _____

Account Name: _____

Website : _____

User I.D. : _____

Email Used : _____

Password : _____

Notes :

Notes :

Account Name: _____

Website : _____

User I.D. : _____

Email Used : _____

Password : _____

Account Name: _____

Website : _____

User I.D. : _____

Email Used : _____

Password : _____

Notes :

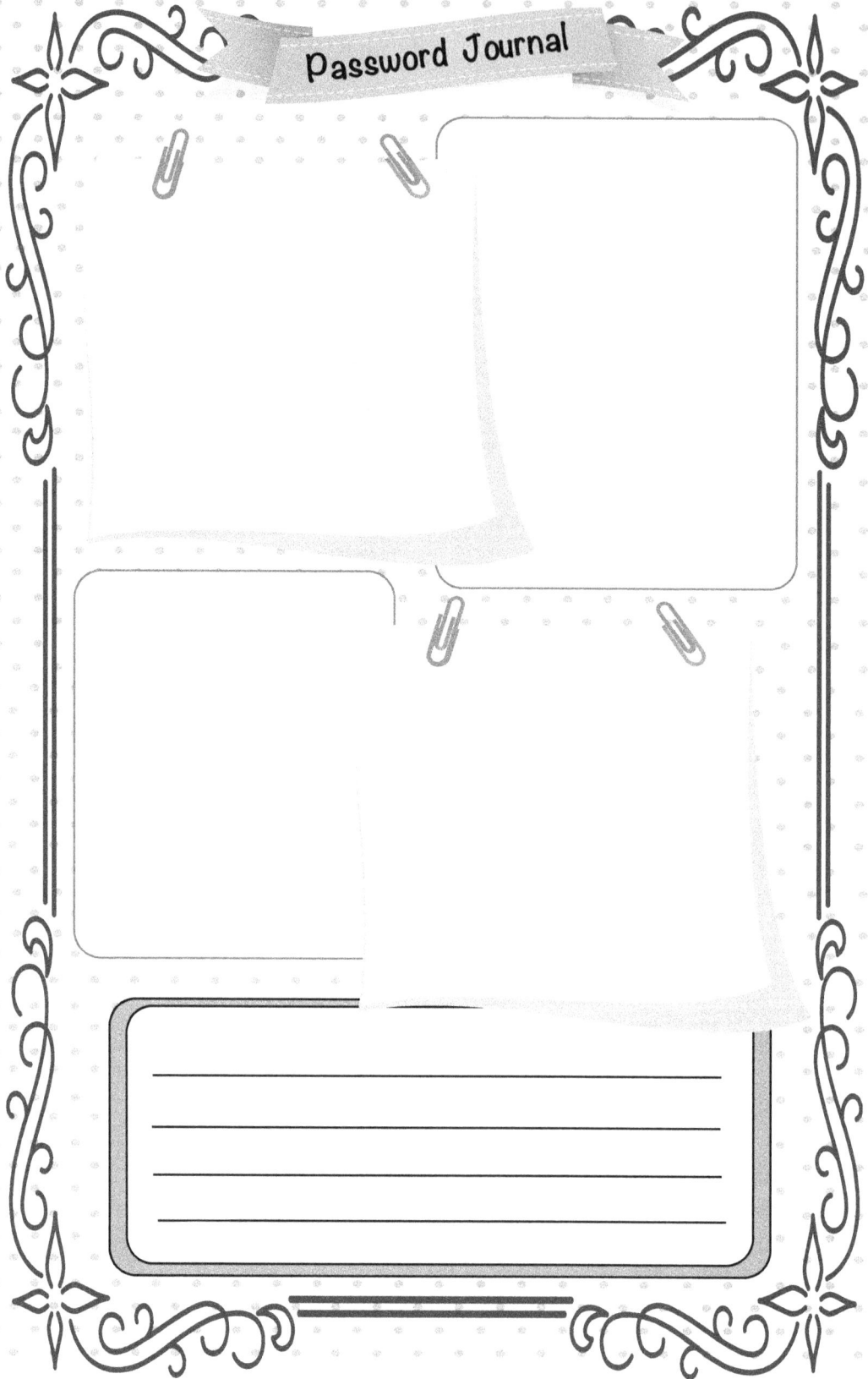

Password Journal

Notes :

Account Name: _____

Website : _____

User I.D. : _____

Email Used : _____

Password : _____

Account Name: _____

Website : _____

User I.D. : _____

Email Used : _____

Password : _____

Notes :

Notes :

Account Name: _____

Website : _____

User I.D. : _____

Email Used : _____

Password : _____

Account Name: _____

Website : _____

User I.D. : _____

Email Used : _____

Password : _____

Notes :

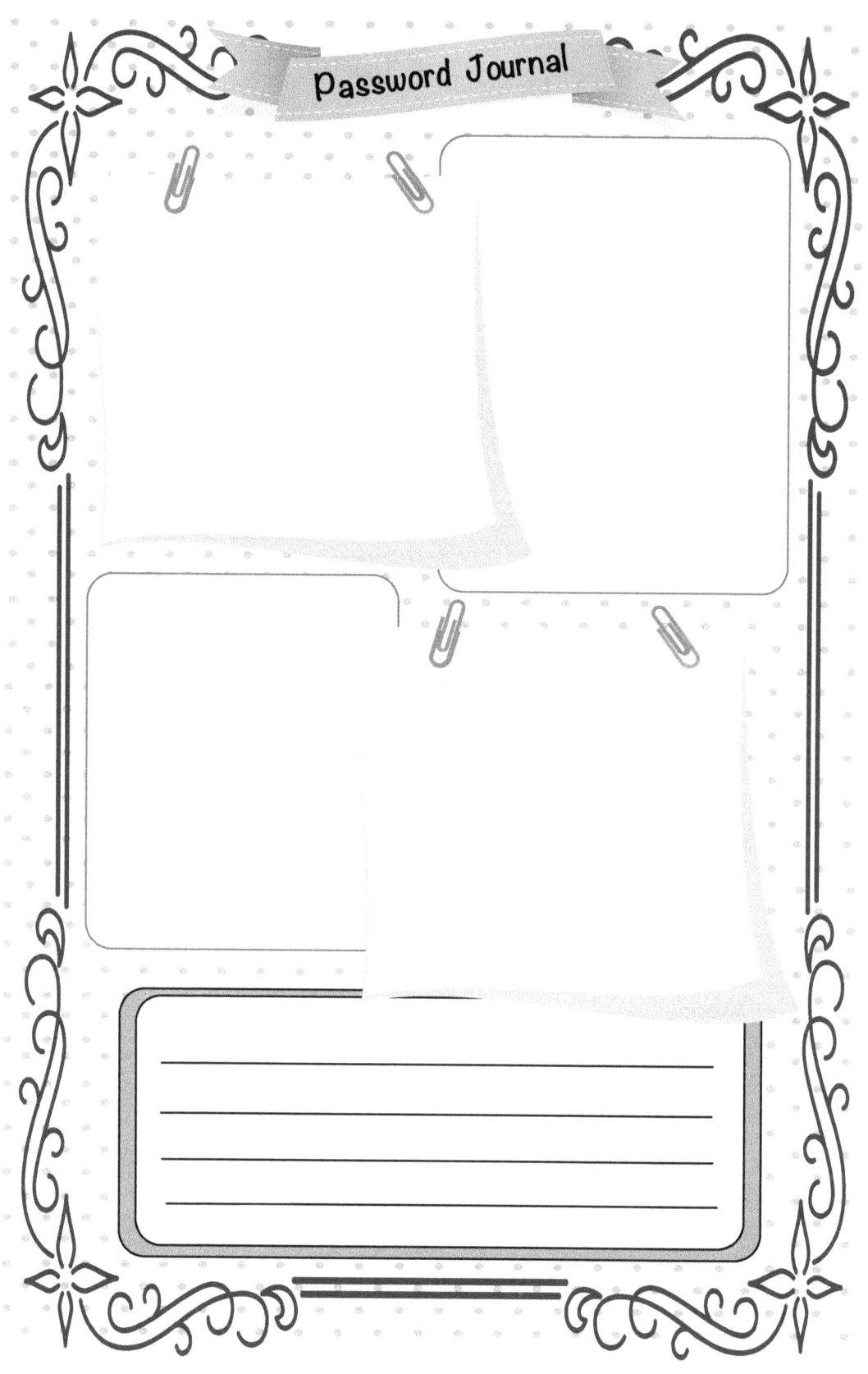

Password Journal

Notes :

Account Name: _____

Website : _____

User I.D. : _____

Email Used : _____

Password : _____

Account Name: _____

Website : _____

User I.D. : _____

Email Used : _____

Password : _____

Notes :

Notes :

Account Name: _____

Website : _____

User I.D. : _____

Email Used : _____

Password : _____

Account Name: _____

Website : _____

User I.D. : _____

Email Used : _____

Password : _____

Notes :

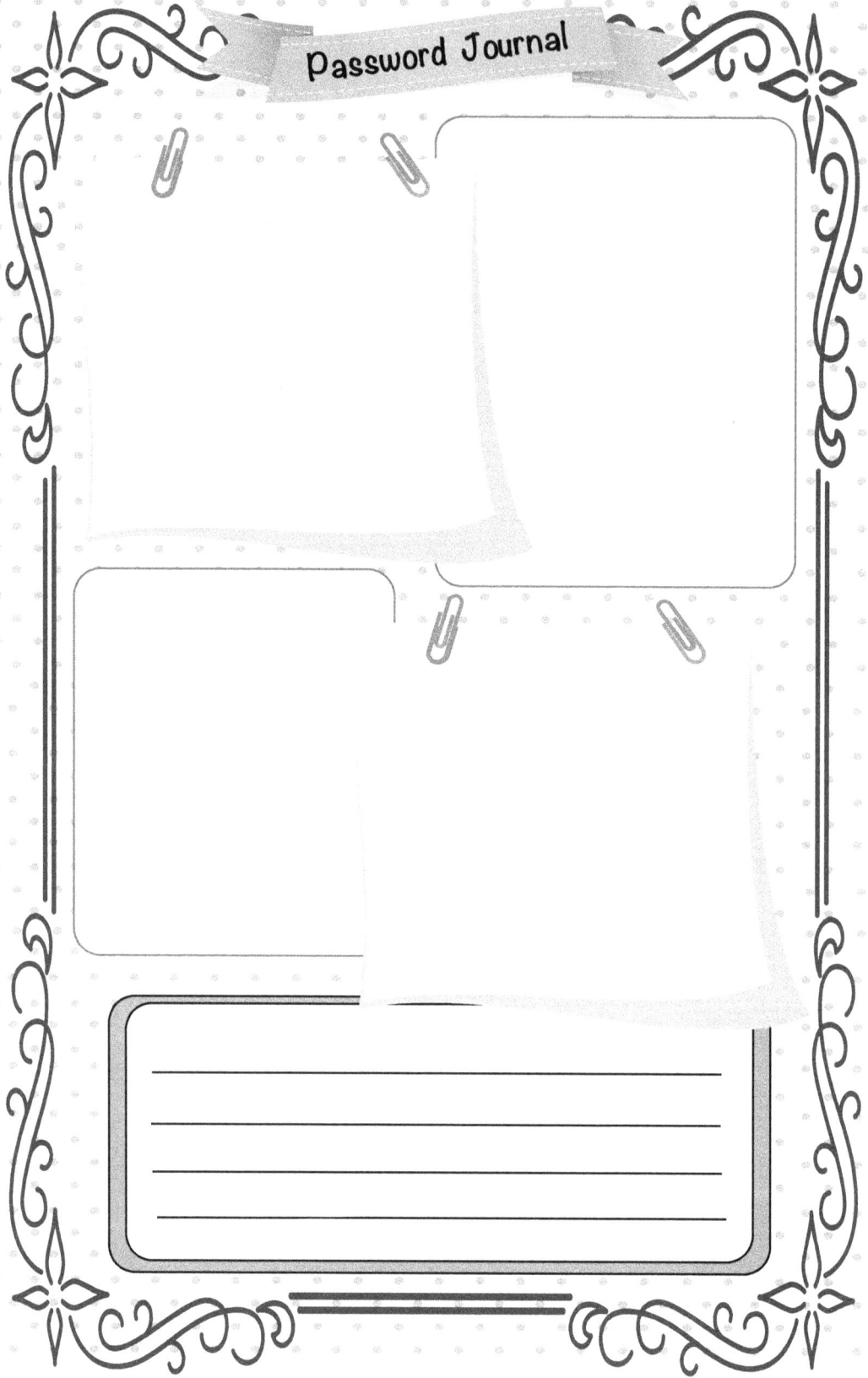

Password Journal

Notes :

Account Name: _____

Website : _____

User I.D. : _____

Email Used : _____

Password : _____

Account Name: _____

Website : _____

User I.D. : _____

Email Used : _____

Password : _____

Notes :

Notes :

Account Name: _____

Website : _____

User I.D. : _____

Email Used : _____

Password : _____

Account Name: _____

Website : _____

User I.D. : _____

Email Used : _____

Password : _____

Notes :

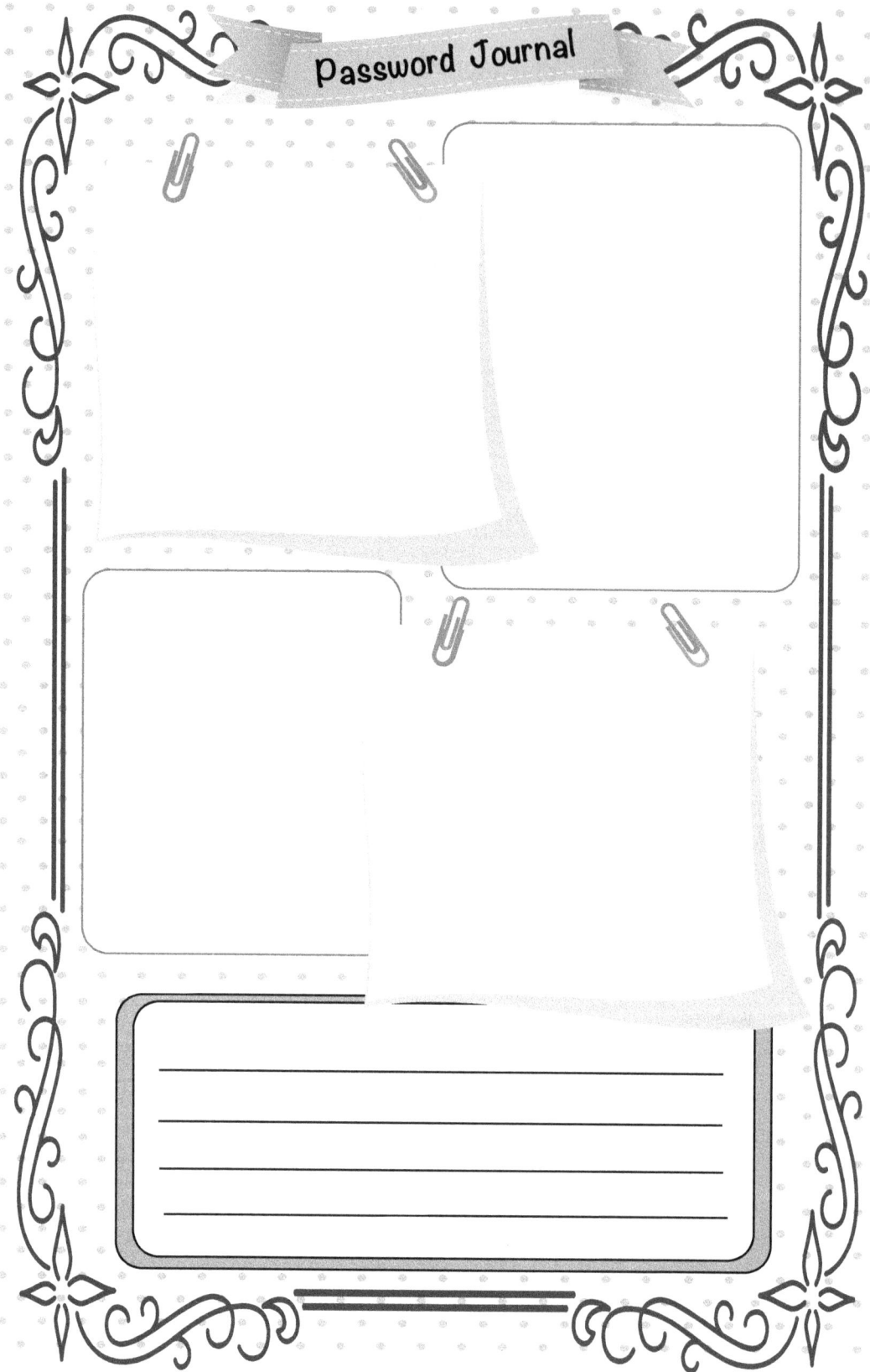

Password Journal

Notes :

Account Name: _____

Website : _____

User I.D. : _____

Email Used : _____

Password : _____

Account Name: _____

Website : _____

User I.D. : _____

Email Used : _____

Password : _____

Notes :

Notes :

Account Name: _____

Website : _____

User I.D. : _____

Email Used : _____

Password : _____

Account Name: _____

Website : _____

User I.D. : _____

Email Used : _____

Password : _____

Notes :

Password Journal

Password Journal

Notes :

Account Name: _____

Website : _____

User I.D. : _____

Email Used : _____

Password : _____

Account Name: _____

Website : _____

User I.D. : _____

Email Used : _____

Password : _____

Notes :

Notes :

Account Name: _____

Website : _____

User I.D. : _____

Email Used : _____

Password : _____

Account Name: _____

Website : _____

User I.D. : _____

Email Used : _____

Password : _____

Notes :

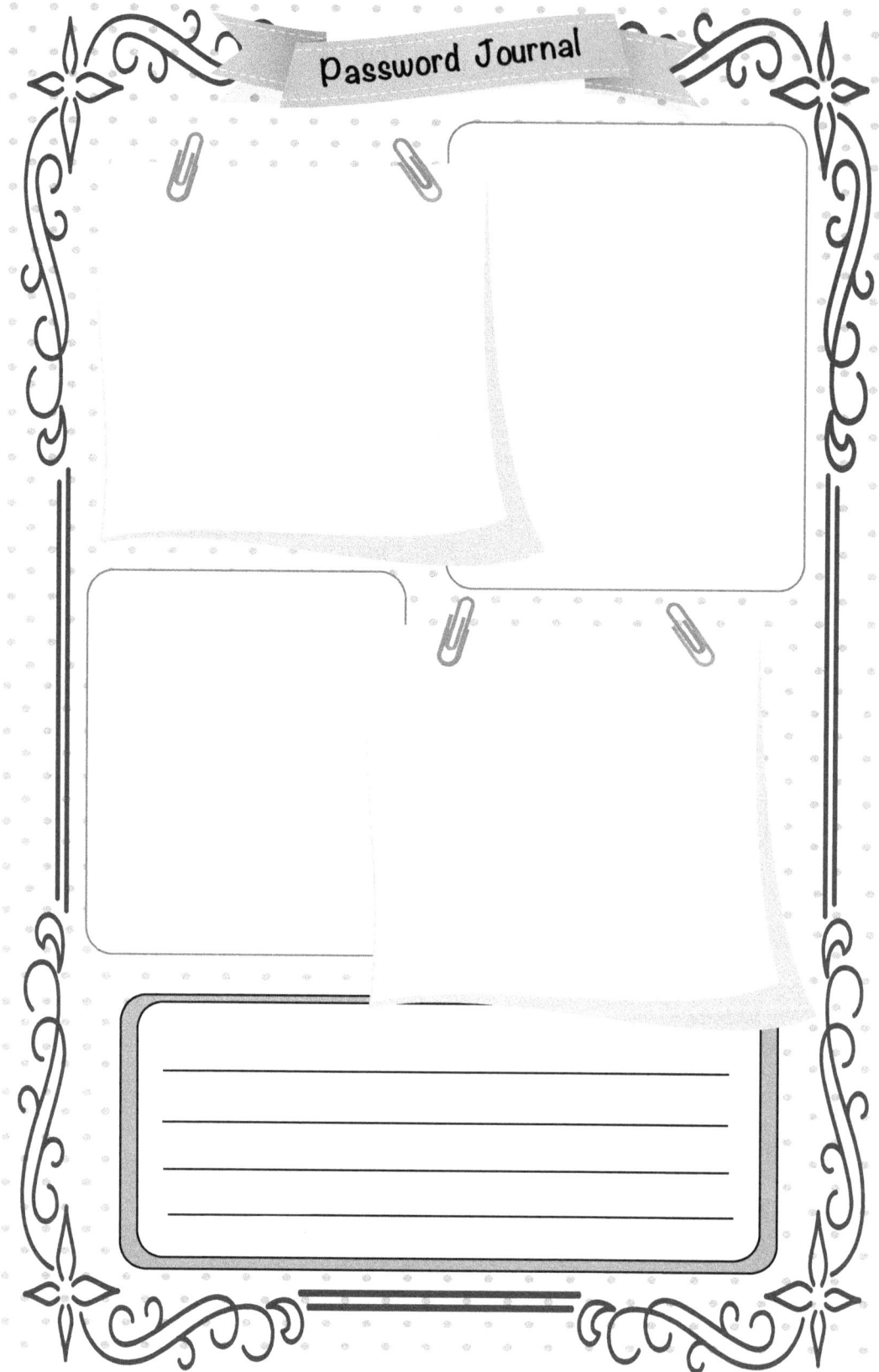

Password Journal

Notes :

Account Name: _____

Website : _____

User I.D. : _____

Email Used : _____

Password : _____

Account Name: _____

Website : _____

User I.D. : _____

Email Used : _____

Password : _____

Notes :

Notes :

Account Name: _____

Website : _____

User I.D. : _____

Email Used : _____

Password : _____

Account Name: _____

Website : _____

User I.D. : _____

Email Used : _____

Password : _____

Notes :

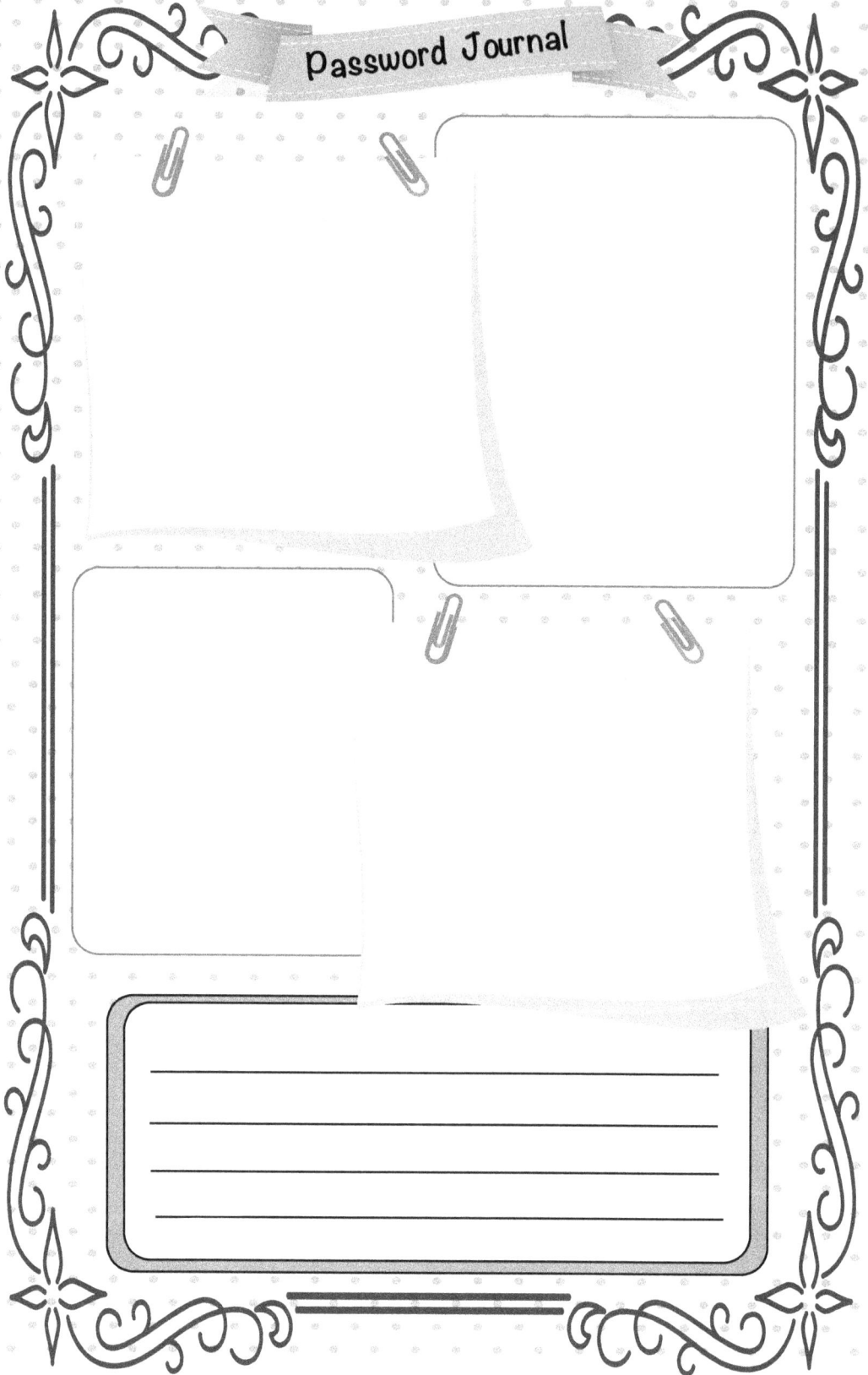

Password Journal

Notes :

Account Name: _____

Website : _____

User I.D. : _____

Email Used : _____

Password : _____

Account Name: _____

Website : _____

User I.D. : _____

Email Used : _____

Password : _____

Notes :

Notes :

Account Name: _____

Website : _____

User I.D. : _____

Email Used : _____

Password : _____

Account Name: _____

Website : _____

User I.D. : _____

Email Used : _____

Password : _____

Notes :

Password Journal

Notes :

Account Name: _____

Website : _____

User I.D. : _____

Email Used : _____

Password : _____

Account Name: _____

Website : _____

User I.D. : _____

Email Used : _____

Password : _____

Notes :

Notes :

Account Name: _____

Website : _____

User I.D. : _____

Email Used : _____

Password : _____

Account Name: _____

Website : _____

User I.D. : _____

Email Used : _____

Password : _____

Notes :

Password Journal

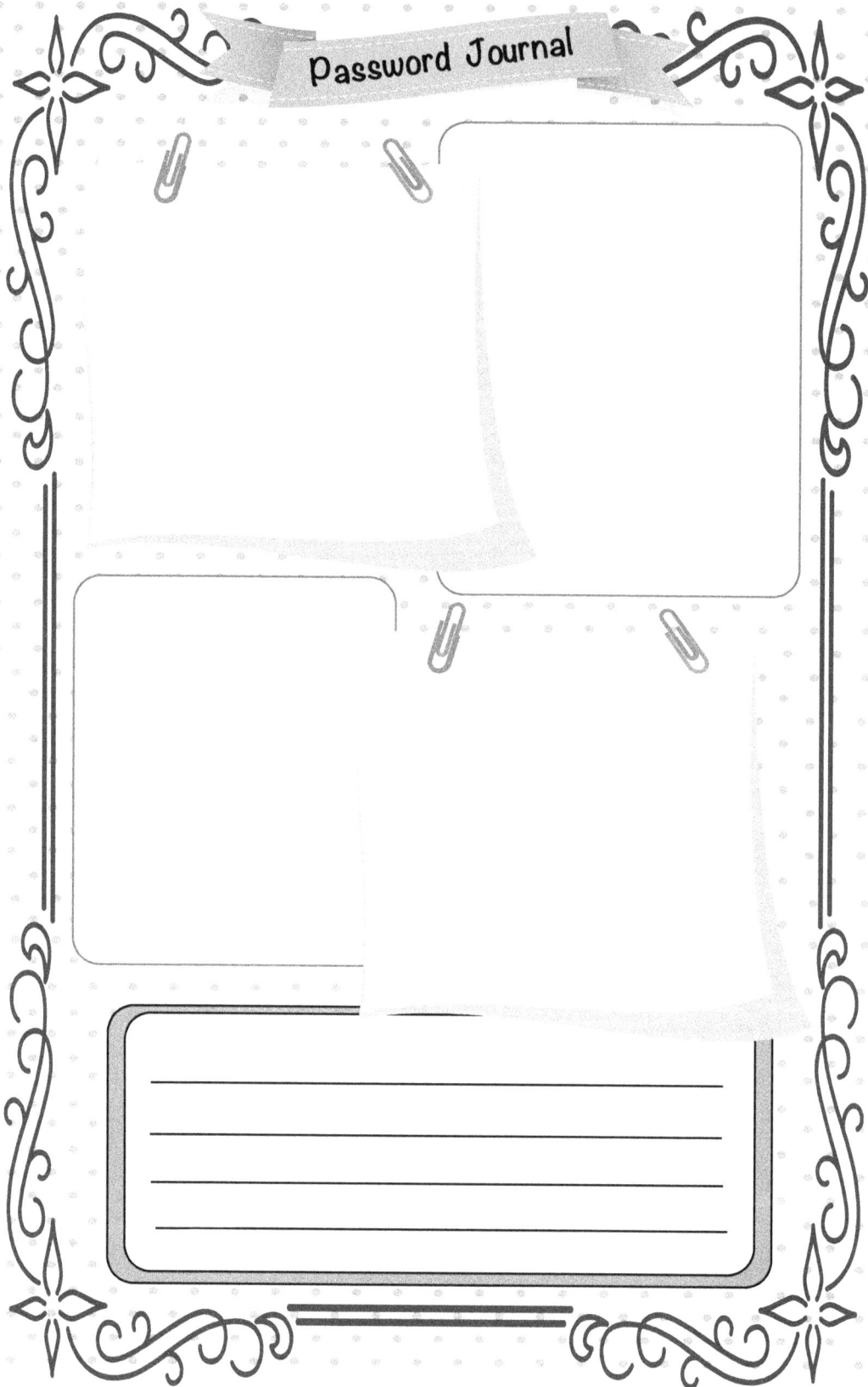

Password Journal

Notes :

Account Name: _____

Website : _____

User I.D. : _____

Email Used : _____

Password : _____

Account Name: _____

Website : _____

User I.D. : _____

Email Used : _____

Password : _____

Notes :

Notes :

Account Name: _____

Website : _____

User I.D. : _____

Email Used : _____

Password : _____

Account Name: _____

Website : _____

User I.D. : _____

Email Used : _____

Password : _____

Notes :

Password Journal

Notes :

Account Name: _____

Website : _____

User I.D. : _____

Email Used : _____

Password : _____

Account Name: _____

Website : _____

User I.D. : _____

Email Used : _____

Password : _____

Notes :

Notes :

Account Name: _____

Website : _____

User I.D. : _____

Email Used : _____

Password : _____

Account Name: _____

Website : _____

User I.D. : _____

Email Used : _____

Password : _____

Notes :

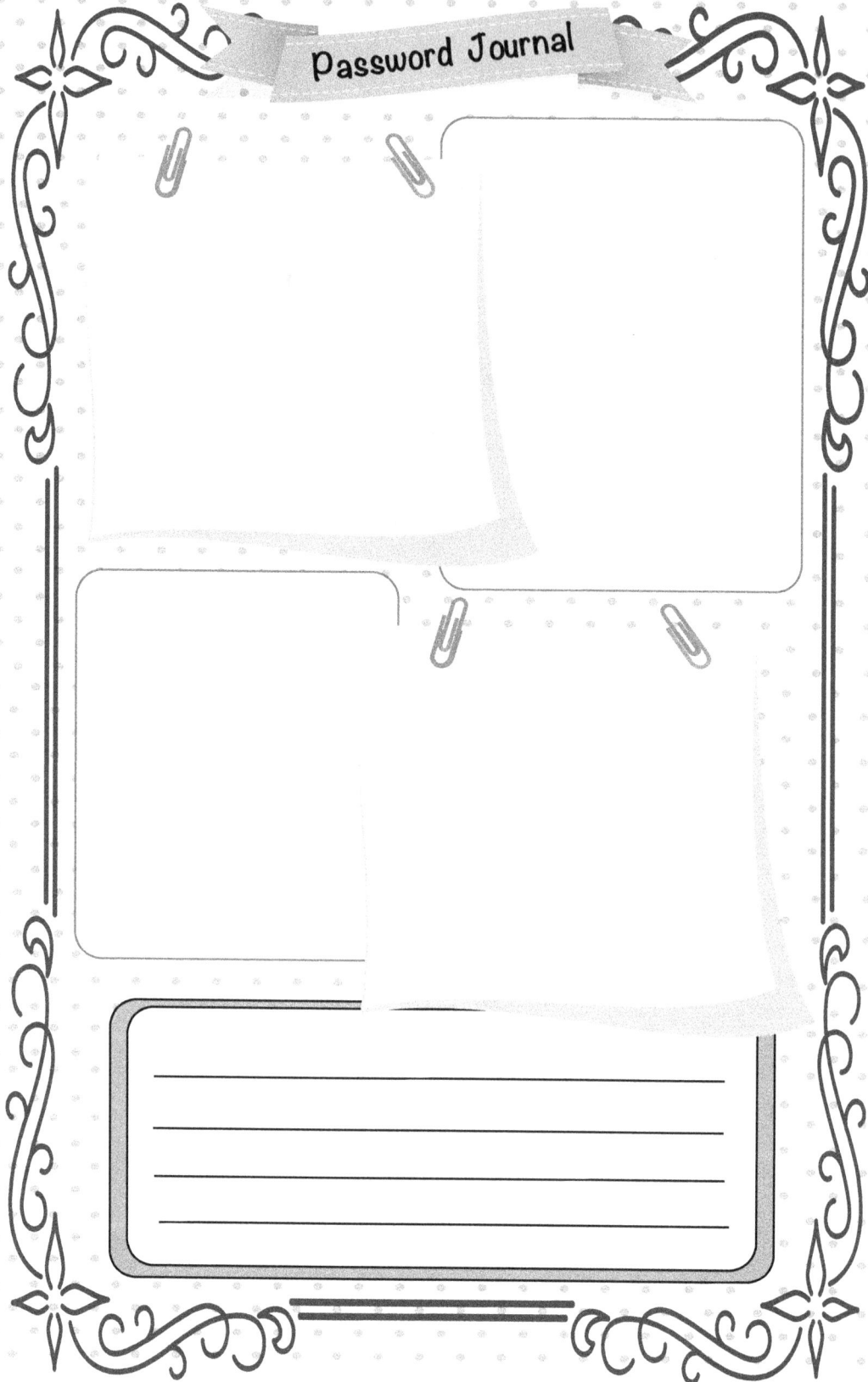

Password Journal

Notes :

Account Name: _____

Website : _____

User I.D. : _____

Email Used : _____

Password : _____

Account Name: _____

Website : _____

User I.D. : _____

Email Used : _____

Password : _____

Notes :

Notes :

Account Name: _____

Website : _____

User I.D. : _____

Email Used : _____

Password : _____

Account Name: _____

Website : _____

User I.D. : _____

Email Used : _____

Password : _____

Notes :

Password Journal

Notes :

Account Name: _____

Website : _____

User I.D. : _____

Email Used : _____

Password : _____

Account Name: _____

Website : _____

User I.D. : _____

Email Used : _____

Password : _____

Notes :

Notes :

Account Name: _____

Website : _____

User I.D. : _____

Email Used : _____

Password : _____

Account Name: _____

Website : _____

User I.D. : _____

Email Used : _____

Password : _____

Notes :

Password Journal

Notes :

Account Name: _____

Website : _____

User I.D. : _____

Email Used : _____

Password : _____

Account Name: _____

Website : _____

User I.D. : _____

Email Used : _____

Password : _____

Notes :

Notes :

Account Name: _____

Website : _____

User I.D. : _____

Email Used : _____

Password : _____

Account Name: _____

Website : _____

User I.D. : _____

Email Used : _____

Password : _____

Notes :

Password Journal

Notes :

Account Name: _____

Website : _____

User I.D. : _____

Email Used : _____

Password : _____

Account Name: _____

Website : _____

User I.D. : _____

Email Used : _____

Password : _____

Notes :

Notes :

Account Name: _____

Website : _____

User I.D. : _____

Email Used : _____

Password : _____

Account Name: _____

Website : _____

User I.D. : _____

Email Used : _____

Password : _____

Notes :

Password Journal

Notes :

Account Name: _____

Website : _____

User I.D. : _____

Email Used : _____

Password : _____

Account Name: _____

Website : _____

User I.D. : _____

Email Used : _____

Password : _____

Notes :

Notes :

Account Name: _____

Website : _____

User I.D. : _____

Email Used : _____

Password : _____

Account Name: _____

Website : _____

User I.D. : _____

Email Used : _____

Password : _____

Notes :

Password Journal

Notes :

Account Name: _____

Website : _____

User I.D. : _____

Email Used : _____

Password : _____

Account Name: _____

Website : _____

User I.D. : _____

Email Used : _____

Password : _____

Notes :

Notes :

Account Name: _____

Website : _____

User I.D. : _____

Email Used : _____

Password : _____

Account Name: _____

Website : _____

User I.D. : _____

Email Used : _____

Password : _____

Notes :

Password Journal

Password Journal

Notes :

Account Name: _____

Website : _____

User I.D. : _____

Email Used : _____

Password : _____

Account Name: _____

Website : _____

User I.D. : _____

Email Used : _____

Password : _____

Notes :

Notes :

Account Name: _____

Website : _____

User I.D. : _____

Email Used : _____

Password : _____

Account Name: _____

Website : _____

User I.D. : _____

Email Used : _____

Password : _____

Notes :

Password Journal

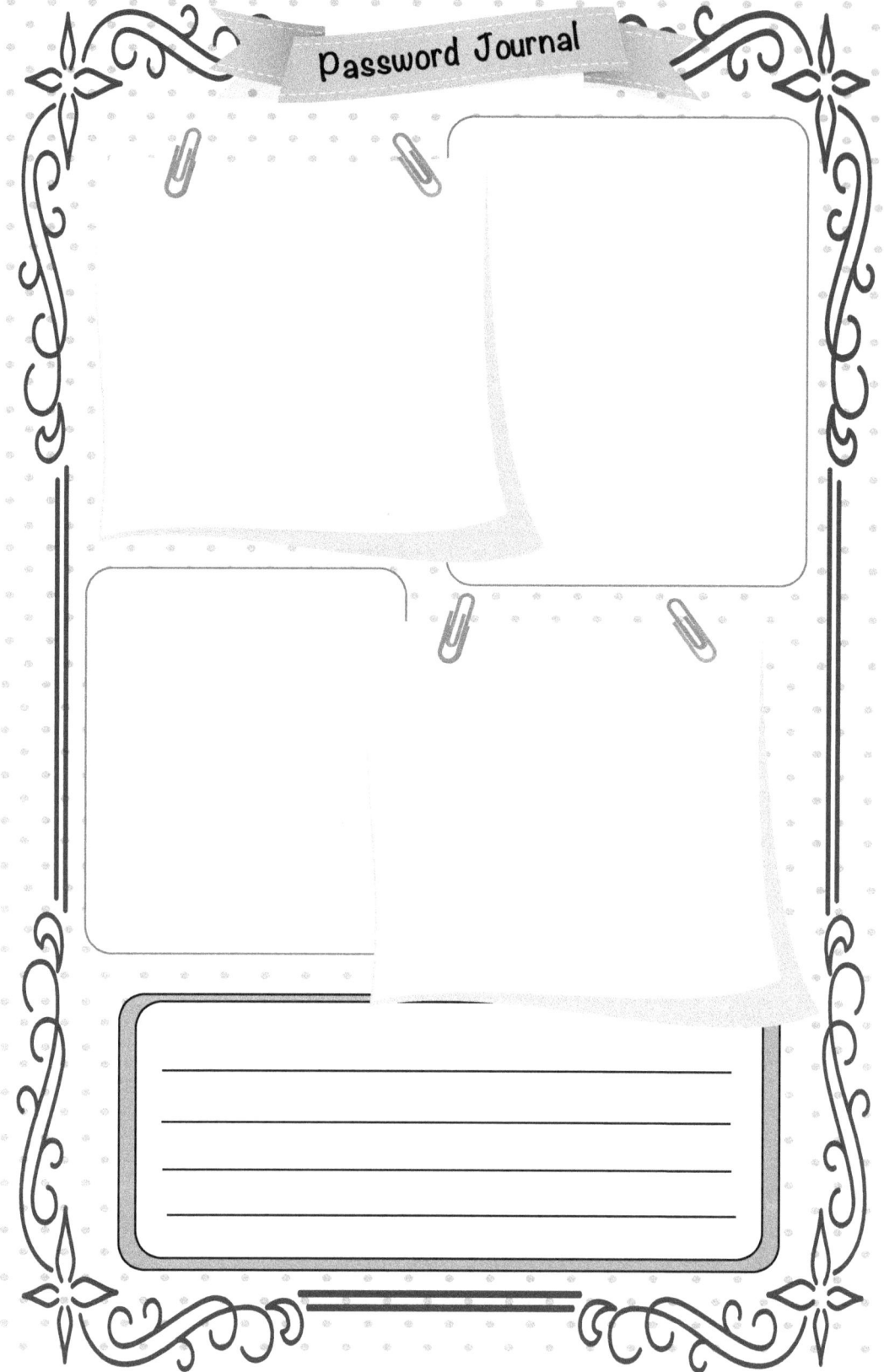

Password Journal

Notes :

Account Name: _____

Website : _____

User I.D. : _____

Email Used : _____

Password : _____

Account Name: _____

Website : _____

User I.D. : _____

Email Used : _____

Password : _____

Notes :

Notes :

Account Name: _____

Website : _____

User I.D. : _____

Email Used : _____

Password : _____

Account Name: _____

Website : _____

User I.D. : _____

Email Used : _____

Password : _____

Notes :

Password Journal

Password Journal

Notes :

Account Name: _____

Website : _____

User I.D. : _____

Email Used : _____

Password : _____

Account Name: _____

Website : _____

User I.D. : _____

Email Used : _____

Password : _____

Notes :

Notes :

Account Name: _____

Website : _____

User I.D. : _____

Email Used : _____

Password : _____

Account Name: _____

Website : _____

User I.D. : _____

Email Used : _____

Password : _____

Notes :

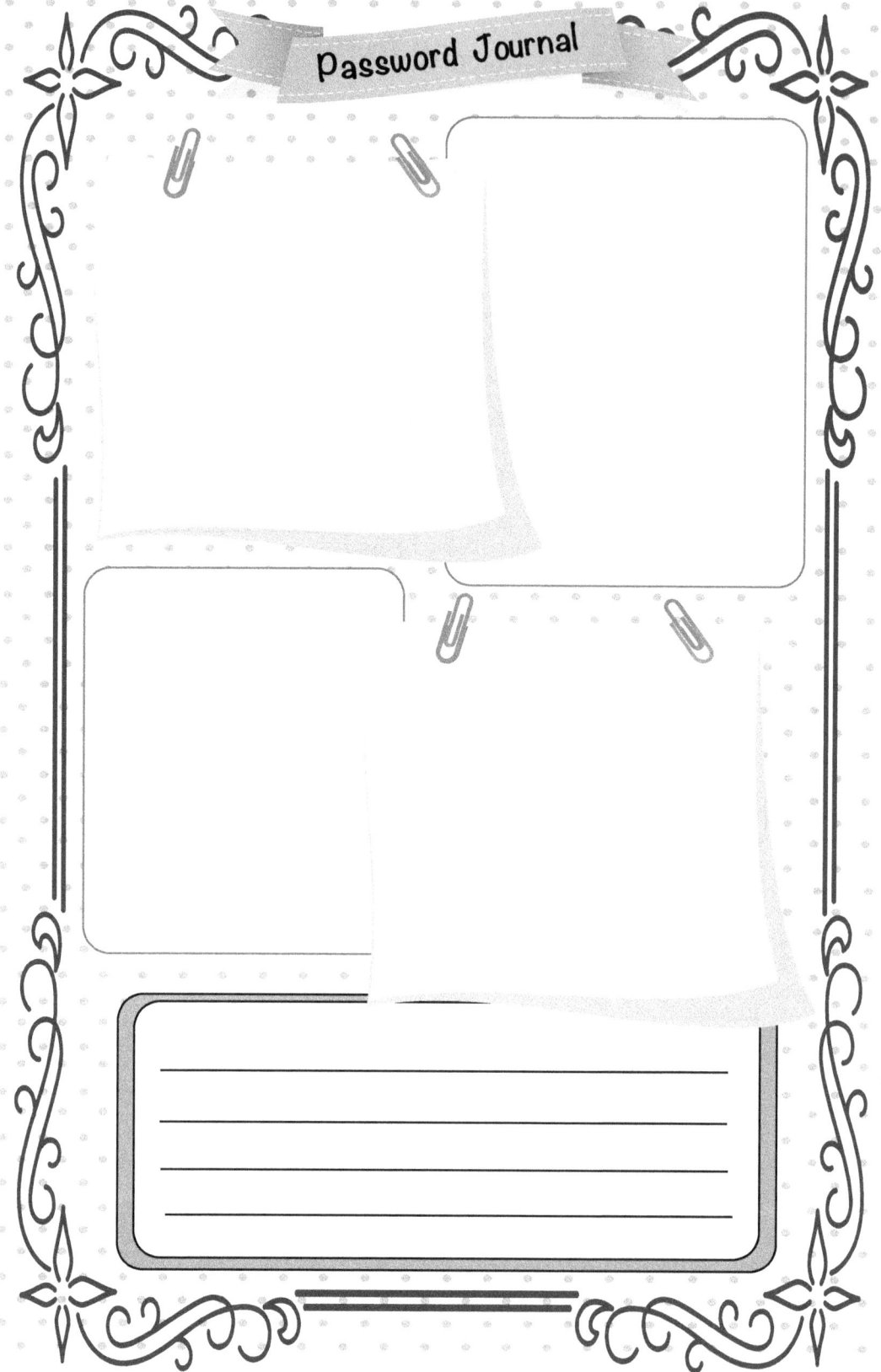

Password Journal

Notes :

Account Name: _____

Website : _____

User I.D. : _____

Email Used : _____

Password : _____

Account Name: _____

Website : _____

User I.D. : _____

Email Used : _____

Password : _____

Notes :

Notes :

Account Name: _____

Website : _____

User I.D. : _____

Email Used : _____

Password : _____

Account Name: _____

Website : _____

User I.D. : _____

Email Used : _____

Password : _____

Notes :

Password Journal

Notes :

Account Name: _____

Website : _____

User I.D. : _____

Email Used : _____

Password : _____

Account Name: _____

Website : _____

User I.D. : _____

Email Used : _____

Password : _____

Notes :

Notes :

Account Name: _____

Website : _____

User I.D. : _____

Email Used : _____

Password : _____

Account Name: _____

Website : _____

User I.D. : _____

Email Used : _____

Password : _____

Notes :

Password Journal

Password Journal

Notes :

Account Name: _____

Website : _____

User I.D. : _____

Email Used : _____

Password : _____

Account Name: _____

Website : _____

User I.D. : _____

Email Used : _____

Password : _____

Notes :

Notes :

Account Name: _____

Website : _____

User I.D. : _____

Email Used : _____

Password : _____

Account Name: _____

Website : _____

User I.D. : _____

Email Used : _____

Password : _____

Notes :

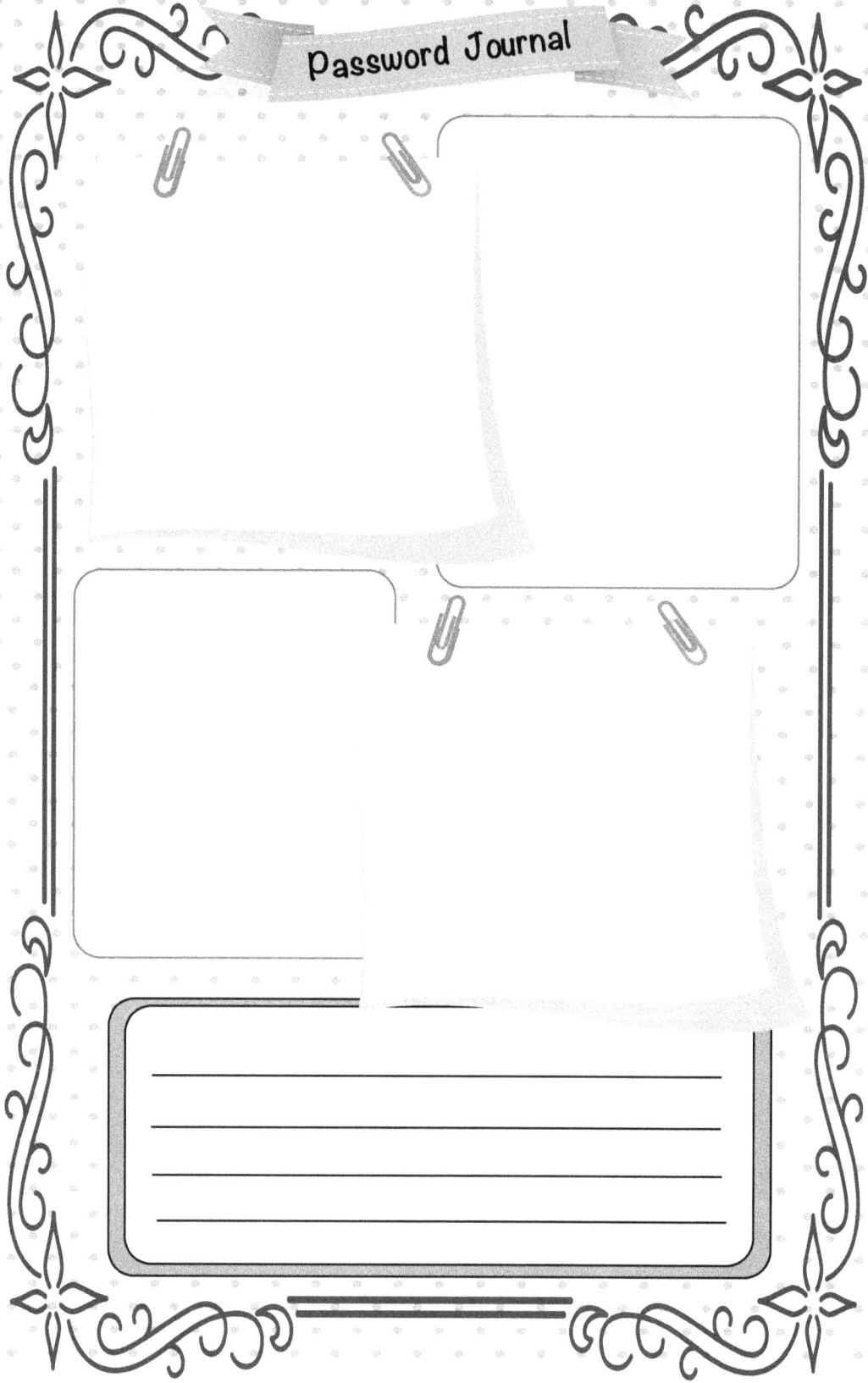

Password Journal

Notes :

Account Name: _____

Website : _____

User I.D. : _____

Email Used : _____

Password : _____

Account Name: _____

Website : _____

User I.D. : _____

Email Used : _____

Password : _____

Notes :

Notes :

Account Name: _____

Website : _____

User I.D. : _____

Email Used : _____

Password : _____

Account Name: _____

Website : _____

User I.D. : _____

Email Used : _____

Password : _____

Notes :

Password Journal

Password Journal

Notes :

Account Name: _____

Website : _____

User I.D. : _____

Email Used : _____

Password : _____

Account Name: _____

Website : _____

User I.D. : _____

Email Used : _____

Password : _____

Notes :

Notes :

Account Name: _____

Website : _____

User I.D. : _____

Email Used : _____

Password : _____

Account Name: _____

Website : _____

User I.D. : _____

Email Used : _____

Password : _____

Notes :

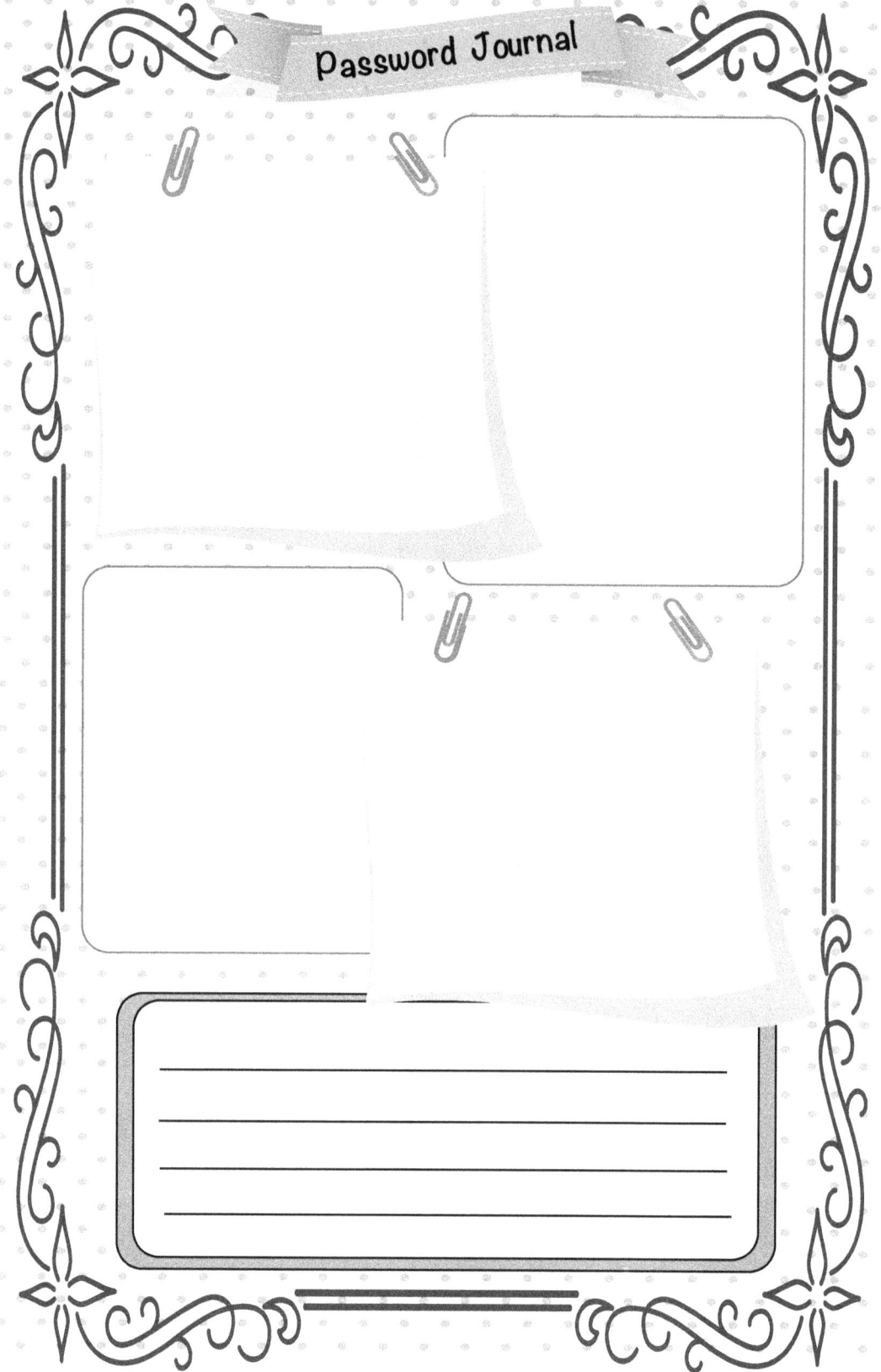

Password Journal

Notes :

Account Name: _____

Website : _____

User I.D. : _____

Email Used : _____

Password : _____

Account Name: _____

Website : _____

User I.D. : _____

Email Used : _____

Password : _____

Notes :

Notes :

Account Name: _____

Website : _____

User I.D. : _____

Email Used : _____

Password : _____

Account Name: _____

Website : _____

User I.D. : _____

Email Used : _____

Password : _____

Notes :

Password Journal

Notes :

Account Name: _____

Website : _____

User I.D. : _____

Email Used : _____

Password : _____

Account Name: _____

Website : _____

User I.D. : _____

Email Used : _____

Password : _____

Notes :

Notes :

Account Name: _____

Website : _____

User I.D. : _____

Email Used : _____

Password : _____

Account Name: _____

Website : _____

User I.D. : _____

Email Used : _____

Password : _____

Notes :

Password Journal

Notes :

Account Name: _____

Website : _____

User I.D. : _____

Email Used : _____

Password : _____

Account Name: _____

Website : _____

User I.D. : _____

Email Used : _____

Password : _____

Notes :

Notes :

Account Name: _____

Website : _____

User I.D. : _____

Email Used : _____

Password : _____

Account Name: _____

Website : _____

User I.D. : _____

Email Used : _____

Password : _____

Notes :

Notes

www.ingramcontent.com/pod-product-compliance
Lightning Source LLC
Chambersburg PA
CBHW081335090426
42737CB00017B/3155